D0801617

THINK ON
THESE THINGS

JOHN C. MAXWELL

THINK ON THESE THINGS

MEDITATIONS FOR LEADERS

30th ANNIVERSARY EDITION

Finally, brethren, whatsoever things are true, whatsoever things are honest, whatsoever things are just, whatsoever things are pure, whatsoever things are lovely, whatsoever things are of good report; if there be any virtue, and if there be any praise, think on these things (Phil. 4:8, KJV).

BEACON HILL PRESS
OF KANSAS CITY

Copyright 1979, 1999, 2009
by Beacon Hill Press of Kansas City
Revised edition 1999
30th anniversary edition 2009

ISBN 978-0-8341-2500-1

Printed in the
United States of America

Cover Design: Brandon Hill
Interior Design: Sharon Page

Library of Congress Cataloging-in-Publication Data

Maxwell, John C., 1947-
   Think on these things : meditations for leaders / John C. Maxwell. — 30th anniversary ed.
     p. cm.
   ISBN 978-0-8341-2500-1 (hardcover)
  1. Christian leadership—Prayers and devotions. I. Title.
  BV652.1.M37   2009
  242'.69—dc22

                        2009048727

10 9 8 7 6 5 4 3 2 1

To

Melvin Maxwell

An example of holy living,
a builder of God's kingdom,
an organizer of churches,
a positive thinker,
a wonderful father.

CONTENTS

PREFACE

The idea for writing this book was born in a church growth conference I was conducting. A pastor during a question-and-answer time asked me where I had picked up my knowledge concerning church growth at such a young age. (The extent of knowledge may be questioned, although I agree that my age at the time, 32, was indeed young!) In all fairness to his question, I replied, "I've known many of these principles of success all my life."

At that moment I realized how privileged I was to have such a wonderful heritage. The encouragement of church leaders to write down some of these important principles has been the motivating force behind this book. Hopefully these chapters will be the springboard to more successful living.

INTRODUCTION

How you think determines who you are. That's why Scripture directs us to be careful about where we focus our attention. Philippians 4:8-9 says, "Finally, brothers, whatever is true, whatever is noble, whatever is right, whatever is pure, whatever is lovely, whatever is admirable—if anything is excellent or praiseworthy—think about such things. Whatever you have learned or received or heard from me, or seen in me—put it into practice. And the God of peace will be with you."

It was from my parents, Melvin and Laura Maxwell, that I learned early in life this lesson about thinking right. They are two of the most godly and most positive people I've ever known. In all my years growing up, I never heard them talk negatively about other people. They continually dwell on what is good and live out their beliefs every single day.

That wonderful legacy—and my desire to pass it on to others—is what prompted me write *Think on These Things* 30 years ago. I wanted to pass on what I had received, especially to pastors and other church leaders. I knew that a leader's ability to achieve anything great for God begins in his or her heart and mind.

A lot has happened to me in the last 30 years. God has been very good to me. I was blessed to enjoy 26 years of ministry in the local church. I was able to found The INJOY Group, an organization that partners with pastors across America and around the world. I've had the privilege of speaking to millions of people. And I've also written numerous books. I've grown a lot, but my heart is still the same. I want more than anything else to add value to people in any way I can.

As I sat down to reread this book, I was delighted to see that the principles are as relevant today as they were when I first wrote them. But that shouldn't be a surprise. They're based on the Bible, and Scripture is timeless. My prayer is that these pages will add value to you, that they would help you to focus on what is noble, right, and praiseworthy so that the God of peace will be with you.

Part I
WISDOM FROM THE WORD

1

THINK ON
THESE THINGS

*Finally, brethren, whatsoever things are true, what-
soever things are honest, whatsoever things are just,
whatsoever things are pure, whatsoever things are
lovely, whatsoever things are of good report; if there
be any virtue, and if there be any praise, think on
these things* (Phil. 4:8, KJV).

I consider Phil. 4:8 to be one of the most important verses
in the Bible. What occupies your mind and what you think
means more than anything else in your life. Your thought
life will determine how much you earn, where you live, and
what you become in life.

Your life today is a result of your thinking yesterday. Your life tomorrow will be determined by what you think today. During a question-and-answer period in a recent ministerial conference, a pastor spoke up and said, "I think I can build a church to average 200. What do you think?"

I said, "I agree—you can build one to that size."

Another pastor, without raising his hand, blurted out, "I think I can build a church up to 500. What do you think?"

I replied, "I agree—you can build a church up to that size."

The first pastor stood up and said, "That doesn't seem fair. Why do you think he can build a larger church than I can when you don't even know our abilities and talents?"

What enters our mind and occupies our thought process will somewhere, sometime come out of our mouth.

My reply to the protesting pastor was, "It doesn't matter which of you has the greater ability. That which determines the success of your church's growth more than any other ingredient is what you *think* you can do. If you think you can, you can. If you think you are, you are."

Words have never been more true than those of the proverb "As he thinks in his heart, so is he" (Prov. 23:7, NKJV).

We've all heard the comment about a man who lacks tact in his conversation: "He says what he thinks." That comment could be made about each of us as well. Although we may not instantly blurt out our initial reactions, they will come out sooner or later if we continue to think about them. What enters our mind and occupies our thought process will somewhere, sometime come out of our mouth.

My father is an example of the preceding statement. He has been successful in church leadership throughout his adult life, as a pastor, district superintendent, and for many years as president of Circleville Bible College. One of the reasons for his success has been his ability to study and concentrate on church-related subjects. Since this specific area has occupied his thinking process for several decades, he opens his mouth, and out come church growth principles. He has become what he thinks about.

It has been said, "Be careful about what you set your heart on, for you'll surely get it." Be careful about what occupies your mind, because it will greatly determine what you'll become tomorrow.

Much of my counseling with people centers on their desire to make changes in their lives. I share with them a simple two-step formula that will help make each one a different person.

First, I have them read 2 Cor. 5:17—"Therefore if any man be in Christ, he is a new creature: old things are passed away; behold, all things are become new" (KJV). The new birth that Jesus said we all must experience to be assured of going to heaven not only determines our eternal destiny but also changes our life right now. Forgiveness of sins removes much heartache and all guilt from the past. The love, joy, and peace that Jesus gives when one becomes His child will without question make a change in any individual's life.

But I know many Christians who still need radical transitions in their homes and in their daily lives. The second step to becoming the person you want to be is changing your thought life. You can literally change your life by beginning to think different thoughts. If you desire a mental "spring cleaning," I suggest you check the following areas.

1. *In what type of environment do you live?*

Each one of us is a product of the environment that surrounds our lives. It is no accident that people who tend to be negative are often found in the same household. Two people can live in the same county, under the same law, with the same privileges, and yet turn out to be drastically different in their values, priorities, and lifestyles. Why? Because their environment, especially at home, was drastically different. Their thoughts reflected what they were given by their environment.

2. *What are you doing in your free time?*

How you spend the time that is your own will greatly determine what you think about. No doubt about it—Satan brings his greatest temptations to people when they have time on their hands. It takes discipline of character and proper goals to handle correctly the extra hours given to an individual in our society.

My parents were very concerned about what we children did in our spare time while we were growing up. They were careful to make sure my brother, sister, and I had plenty of games at home so that our friends could come to our house to play. This enabled them to watch over our activities and relationships. I will forever be indebted to them for encouraging me to read the Bible and good Christian material for a half hour daily. They understood the importance of filling my free time with tools that would help me think right.

3. *Who are your closest friends?*

The people you associate with will greatly determine how you think. One of the positive values of attending church is that the Christian receives encouragement from other believers there. It's possible to know the characteristics of a person by knowing his or her friends. Peer pressure is often the greatest influence upon the life of an individual.

To sum it all up, you can change your life by changing your thinking. You can change your thinking by changing your environment, the use of your free time, and your associations. Use Phil. 4:8 as the guideline to be applied in your thought life. Do your best to make it your standard for selecting friends, filling your free time, and changing your surroundings.

2

WHO KNOCKED A HOLE IN THE ROOF?

One of my favorite Bible stories is recorded in Mark 2:1-12. Jesus had just completed His tour of the synagogues and had returned to Capernaum. The news that Jesus was in town, staying at a certain house, spread quickly through the city. The crowd hurriedly came, and soon the house was jammed full of people waiting to hear Jesus.

Among those with keen interest in seeing Jesus were four men bringing their physically handicapped friend on a stretcher. When they saw that the house was crowded with people, they climbed to the roof and knocked a hole in it so they could lower their friend close to Jesus.

These four men were extraordinary. Every time I think of this story I ask myself, "What kind of people would knock a hole in the roof?" Allow me to suggest some characteristics of such persons:

1. *Concern for others.*

Unselfishness was a characteristic that marked these men. To bring a sick friend to Jesus meant denying themselves many of the blessings others would receive. It meant giving up a front-row seat for a friend, caring enough to be inconvenienced. The beauty of genuine concern is its willingness to become involved without being influenced by the price tag.

2. *The spirit of cooperation.*

It took all four of them to bring their friend to Jesus. Each man realized the importance of the other. Success would be achieved only if every man continued to hold up his part of the bed. Failure was inevitable if any one of them decided to do his own thing.

Coming together is the beginning; working together produces victory.

This truth is underlined in the story of the people of Israel fighting against the Amalekites in the wilderness (Exod. 17). When their leader, Moses, stretched his hands toward heaven, the Israelites would advance toward victory.

When his hands and arms became so tired that they fell to his side, the Amalekites started advancing. Aaron and Hur realized that victory would be possible only with their cooperation. With team spirit they both grasped Moses' hands and held them high toward heaven until victory was won.

It would be profitable for each one of us to realize that we need each other. Coming together is the beginning; working together produces victory.

3. A firm belief that the only answer is Jesus.

The conviction that only Jesus could take care of their friend's problem gave the men boldness and determination. They could have said, "He's too heavy" or "The crowd is too large" or "We have lost our opportunity." They could have gone home discouraged and missed a miracle—but they refused to quit.

When former heavyweight champion James J. Corbett was asked what it took to go to the top, he replied, "Fight one more round." Then he added, "When your feet are so tired that you have to shuffle back to the center of the ring, fight one more round." The determination of four men meant victory for their friend.

4. Having priorities straight.

These men knew that the most important thing in the world at the moment was to bring their friend to Jesus.

Therefore, up on the roof they went. No doubt they were besieged by thoughts such as, "This will disturb the service"; "We've never done anything like this before"; "What will people think?" Yet they would not stop—they *could* not stop. Why? They had a job to do that was greater than the threat of being different.

Thank God for the people who are willing to knock holes in roofs. They are the pacesetters, the barrier-breakers, the miracle-producers. They are different because they are determined. They're criticized because they're concerned. But most important—they bring people to Jesus.

3

WHO PATCHED UP
THE ROOF?

When Jesus touched the lame man in Capernaum, no doubt there was much rejoicing. The sick man was healed, took his bed, and walked home to a happy family. His four friends experienced the thrill that comes in helping others. The crowd who gathered to see Jesus was certainly not disappointed.

However, a question persists in my mind. After all the excitement, the miracles, the rejoicing, and the praising of Jesus—who patched up the roof? To find the answer, let us look at the other side of the coin: Who did *not* patch up the roof?

1. *The various onlookers didn't patch up the roof.*

They just saw the crowd and decided to stick around for a while to see what would happen. They weren't involved in Christ's work. Curiosity, not Christ, attracted them.

2. *The critical scribes didn't patch up the roof.*

The Bible says they didn't work. Their trademark was a critical spirit. Their interest was not in building up the kingdom of our Lord; they were trying to blow it up.

3. *The "Bless-Me Club" didn't patch up the roof.*

This group of people, who are always wanting a thrill without paying the bill, were not disciplined enough to be away from the excitement. They wanted to follow Jesus only so they could witness another miracle.

4. *Those who were amazed at Jesus' miracle didn't patch up the roof.*

Their amazement probably spilled over into the streets of the city, where they excitedly told their friends about the great things Jesus had done. Their amazement and their desire to share it couldn't wait for the menial task of repairing a roof.

5. *The average attender didn't help patch up the roof.*

The crowd who came to hear Jesus apparently wouldn't even move out of the way to let the lame man and his friends into the house. If they were so unconcerned that they wouldn't let the men into the building, certainly their lack of compassion would hinder them from fixing the roof. It was the unwillingness to make way for the needy one that forced the men to go to the roof in the first place.

6. *It's not clear that even the four men who knocked a hole in the roof patched it up.*

Why? When Jesus comes and the thrill of being in His presence impresses us, we become excited, turned-on Christians. Within this spiritually charged atmosphere, people sometimes find it natural to do the unusual—like knocking holes in roofs. However, when the excitement dies down, it soon becomes evident that it's much easier to do things like knocking holes in roofs when miracles are about to happen than to patch them up after the miracles have gone.

The person who patched up the roof was someone who served Jesus *because of who He was rather than because of what He did.* This type of person appreciates the message more than the miracles, the life more than the loaves, the truth more than the thrills. You occasionally find this type of individual in the church today. He or she is always a blessing. Faithfulness, loyalty, and dependability are trademarks of this individual's life. When the shouting has subsided and the excitement has died down, he or she is ready to pick up the pieces and do the dirty work.

The person who patched up the roof was someone who followed Jesus, knowing that the cross comes before the crown. This person has counted the cost. He or she has embraced and accepted the principle Jesus enunciated: "Whoever loses his life for me will find it" (Matt. 16:25).

Unquestionably, God's kingdom is being advanced by people of little talent doing little jobs for a big God.

Finally, the person who patched up the roof after the crowd left certainly loved Jesus enough to think that no job is insignificant. Unquestionably, God's kingdom is being advanced by people of little talent doing little jobs for a big God. It's exciting to know that God needs every roof-patcher He can find. The individual who is disciplined enough to do the unexciting and devoted enough to do the uninteresting will certainly find patching up roofs rewarding in God's work.

4

I COULDN'T
CARE MORE

I was awakened by a persistent knock on my motel room door at 3:45 A.M. It was the police! Immediately negative thoughts rushed into my mind: "Here I am in Chicago holding a conference, and something bad has happened back home." How relieved I was to discover that I was wrong! The police were looking for a lady who had threatened to commit suicide.

Sure enough, a young lady in a nearby room lay in desperation on a bed crying out to die. Quickly the police held her down to the bed until her feet and hands were securely handcuffed. For the next 45 minutes I listened to her cry over and over again, "Please let me die! Let me alone! Nobody cares! Nobody loves me!"

The rest of that night I thought about the desperation and the agony of that lonely young woman. Somehow the message "I couldn't care less" had echoed through the streets of Chicago until she felt compelled to reject life. How many lives are wasted and destroyed because the world's attitudes and actions toward needy people say, "I couldn't care less"? How beautiful this world would be if this unchristian philosophy were replaced with Christian attitudes until people would begin saying, "I couldn't care more"!

If I'm to say to my world, "I couldn't care more," I must open my eyes and look for hurting people. It's possible for two people to look upon the same situation and see things entirely different. Matthew 9:35-38 tells us that "Jesus was going about all the cities and the villages, teaching in their synagogues, and proclaiming the gospel of the kingdom, and healing every kind of disease and every kind of sickness. And seeing the multitudes, He felt compassion for them, because they were distressed and downcast like sheep without a shepherd. Then He said to His disciples, 'The harvest is plentiful, but the workers are few. Therefore beseech the Lord of the harvest to send out workers into His harvest'" (NASB).

> *If I'm to say to my world, "I couldn't care more," I must open my eyes and look for hurting people.*

Jesus was concerned that people see the hurts of humanity and respond with care. Too many times we, like the disciples, see only the problems of people. We feel the frustration of their failures and the weight of their weaknesses. We remember only the reliance upon *our* strength and forget our obligation to freely give what we have received. The apostle Paul stated in Rom. 15:1-3, "We who are strong ought to bear with the failings of the weak and not to please ourselves. Each of us should please his neighbor for his good, to build him up. For even Christ did not please himself."

If I'm to say to my neighbor, "I couldn't care more," I must open my heart and allow love for others to fill it. First Corinthians 13:3 clearly states that "if I give all I possess to the poor and surrender my body to the flames, but have not love, I gain nothing." My helping hand to a needy world is empty unless love is the motive.

Material handouts are a poor substitute for love and understanding. People don't need more things—they need more tenderness. Sacrifice without love is also pointless. The question is not *what* you die *for* but *why* you die.

Many adults are wandering around the world in the same predicament as the little girl who lived in an orphanage. Each time prospective parents came to the orphanage, the precious little child would hope to be selected. After many times of rejection, she reached up to the latest prospective parents and cried, "Please take me—I just want somebody to love me!" On a crowded city street with thousands of people busily moving about, there are those who inwardly are lonely and looking for somebody who cares.

On one Sunday that stands out in my memory, my heart was broken as I preached to hundreds of needy people. The tears flowed as I tried to share with them God's love. The message was not up to par, from my viewpoint. Yet when the invitation was given for those to come forward who had spiritual needs, dozens responded. One man visiting our church for the first time looked up at me through his tears and said, "Thanks for caring."

I replied, "Sir, I couldn't care more."

5

YOUR REACTION SHOWS YOUR CHRISTIANITY

Jesus said in Matt. 5:43-48,

> You have heard that it was said, "Love your neighbor and hate your enemy." But I tell you: Love your enemies and pray for those who persecute you, that you may be sons of your Father in heaven. He causes his sun to rise on the evil and the good, and sends rain on the righteous and the unrighteous. If you love those who love you, what reward will you get? Are not even the tax collectors doing that? And if you greet only your brothers, what are you doing more than others? Do not even pagans do that? Be perfect, therefore, as your heavenly Father is perfect.

Jesus not only taught this message but lived it. Jesus experienced misunderstanding, ingratitude, and rejection. But He was never bitter, discouraged, or overcome. To Him, every obstacle was an opportunity.

Brokenheartedness? An opportunity to comfort. Disease? An opportunity to heal. Hatred? An opportunity to love. Temptation? An opportunity to overcome. Sin? An opportunity to forgive. His *uncommon* response to the everyday problems caused those around Him to ask, "What manner of man is this?" (KJV).

People are known not by how they act when they're in control, but by how they react when things are beyond their control.

Long ago I learned that people are known not by how they act when they're in control, but by how they *react* when things are *beyond* their control.

How do we react when criticized? There's always someone in the crowd who will criticize. By the way, some people find fault so freely you would think they were getting paid for it. Many people have been hurt under the banner of constructive criticism. Here's an interesting observation: It's constructive criticism when I criticize you; it's *de*structive criticism when *you* criticize *me.*

Whether criticism is unjust or just, a person shows his or her true mettle by how he or she responds. *The best way to lose an enemy is to treat him like a friend.* It would help each of us to realize that there are times we make errors and display shortcomings. In our relationship with our Heavenly Father, we don't need justice—we need mercy. In our relationships with others, we should be quick to give mercy and slow to demand justice.

When tempted to react in an unchristian manner, we should do the following:

1. *Realize that everyone you meet is fighting a hard battle.*

The other person's life is no easier than yours. Perhaps today he or she is lonely, misunderstood, and hurt. A sure indication that a person hurts inside is the confirmation by what he or she says on the outside. Such a person may hurt you by what he or she says or does because of inward hurt.

2. *Reacting in a positive, reassuring manner will produce better results.*

Recently I hit another car while traveling on a four-lane highway. The driver of the other car was frightened and angry. Immediately I apologized, assured her that I had an excellent insurance company, and told the patrolman I was at fault. I made a friend out of the person whose car I had bumped. How? By a positive reaction to a negative situation.

3. *There's no better way to witness for Christ than by your Christian reactions.*

The fruit of the Spirit, as listed in Gal. 5:22-23, is not to be displayed only during the easy times. These attributes are given so that they will become a part of daily life and be in evidence even when things go wrong. If someone is hungry and becomes irritable toward you, give him or her a piece of bread and butter. That's showing kindness. But at the same time, why not spread a little jam on it? That's *loving*kindness. That's the right reaction. That's genuine Christianity.

6

DON'T JUST DO SOMETHING— STAND THERE!

Everyone is busy. Schedules to follow, goals to achieve, problems to solve, appointments to keep, jobs to finish, places to go, kids to love, deadlines to meet. I like keeping busy. I love my work. But sometimes at the end of my day I feel as if I've been riding a merry-go-round. Plenty of action and movement—yet I didn't seem to go anywhere, and when my day is done, I get off where I started. When this happens, I know it's time to take the advice of my good missionary friend Don Seymour: "Don't just do something—stand there."

Today I have heeded that advice. I'm 300 miles from home in a quiet motel room with just my Bible, two books, paper, and a pen. Today is a day for spiritual refreshment. It's a day to slowly digest the Word of God. It's a day to praise and thank Him for His many blessings upon my life. Today is a day for mental relaxation. No schedule to follow, no problems to hear, no telephones to answer, no advice to give, no deadlines to meet.

Today is also a day of physical rest. It's nice for once not to wake up by the sound of an alarm. An afternoon nap is an almost forgotten luxury. I'm beginning to feel refreshed.

Allow me to share with you some of the reasons it's necessary at times to stand still instead of rushing around.

1. *There's a constant need to reevaluate our priorities.*

Paul says in Rom. 12:2, "Don't let the world around you squeeze you into its own mould" (PHILLIPS). It's very easy to fall into step with the world's thinking and put on the world's attitudes about life. The pressure of the crowd sometimes starts us in the wrong direction. It's easy to follow the lines of least resistance. When our lives fail to embrace discipline and our desires become selfish, it's time to stop and reevaluate our lives.

2. *Only by waiting on God can we be spiritually energized.*

Isaiah 40:29-31 says, "He gives strength to the weary

and increases the power of the weak. Even youths grow tired and weary, and young men stumble and fall; but those who hope in the LORD will renew their strength. They will soar on wings like eagles; they will run and not grow weary, they will walk and not be faint."

3. *It's necessary to review the past.*

History is a great teacher. Experience is a hard teacher. Only by taking time to reflect on yesterday and honestly evaluate its successes and failures can you learn and prepare for tomorrow. Your willingness to learn and adjust positively from mistakes and shortcomings will largely determine how far you will travel the road to success.

4. *Problems will begin to resolve more easily when exposed to the light of time.*

If possible, it's always best to give tough situations extra time for creative thinking and effective action.

Only as we stop in meditation will our hearts be filled with praise for our friends, our past blessings, and our God.

5. *Taking time out increases our capacity for gratitude.*

A thankful heart is one that has had time to count blessings. The leper who was cleansed by Jesus was too busy rejoicing to remember to thank Him. Only as we stop in meditation will our hearts be filled with praise for our friends, our past blessings, and our God.

6. *A day's worth of hesitation sometimes is sufficient time to allow the situations around us to change.*

Many problems will take care of themselves if given the opportunity. In an option play in football, the quarterback hesitates just long enough to force the opposing tackler to commit himself. Then he'll know what he should do to make the desired yardage.

7. *Standing still is a great tool used to prepare an individual for the pressures and battles of life.*

Ephesians 6 is the chapter in which the apostle Paul writes about the victorious Christian soldier. Verses 13 and 14 entreat us to "put on the full armor of God, so that when the day of evil comes, you may be able to stand your ground, and after you have done everything, to stand. Stand firm then." The words "stand firm" mean to "hold still." Part of the preparation for the battles of life is not only to acquire the right equipment to wear on the body but also to make proper preparations of the mind. "Hold still" before charging into the activities of life.

8. **Finally, *relaxation and rest are necessary that we might feel, think, and act right.***

Our spiritual, physical, and emotional condition will greatly determine how we react to situations. The better we feel, the more capable we will be to evaluate difficult situations and make important decisions. When pressures are pressing, schedules are screaming, and the world is whirling, don't just do something—stand there!

7

WHAT KIND OF FRUIT IS ON YOUR TREE?

The psalmist wrote concerning the happiness that a Christian possesses. In Ps. 1:3 we read, "He is like a tree planted by streams of water, which yields its fruit in season." Jesus spoke figuratively concerning a tree as representing a person's life when He said, "A tree [man] is recognized by its fruit" (Matt. 12:33). Jesus also said in John 15:8, "This is to my Father's glory, that you bear much fruit, showing yourselves to be my disciples." Since my life has been figuratively illustrated as a tree, I must answer this question: *What kind of fruit is on my tree?*

I know very little about trees. One summer I planted various types of trees in the backyard. Because they had no fruit on them when I placed them in the ground, I could have easily confused one from the other. Therefore I left the tag on each one so I could identify what type each one was.

When those trees began bearing fruit, I no longer needed a tag to identify them. I knew what type they were simply by the fruit they bore.

This is also true of our lives. Those around us know what type of a person we are because of the fruit we bear in our daily living.

Here's a truth that's important to consider: just as a tree can't produce fruit that's not of its kind, neither can we. In other words, we can produce in our lives only fruit that's consistent with our character. No person is such a deceiver that he or she can produce consistently what he or she does not believe or embrace.

Several years ago I read a true story that beautifully illustrates the preceding point. For four decades East Berlin was controlled by the Communists. West Berlin was free. One day some people who lived in East Berlin took a truckload of garbage and dumped it on the West Berlin side. The people of West Berlin could have retaliated by doing the same thing. But instead they took a truckload of canned goods, bread, and milk and neatly stacked it on the East

Berlin side. On top of this stack of food they placed the sign: "Each gives what he has."

What do you have to give? The answer to that question can be found by looking at the type of fruit you're producing. It's sad to realize that many people have needs that very few can meet. The reason? Most individuals concentrate their efforts on picking fruit instead of producing it. It's easier to be a consumer than a contributor. Others have a fear of giving away so much fruit that they'll become barren. That person who lives in fear of sharing too much often finds that the "much" kept for self is too little to live on.

In John 15 Jesus gives the formula for successful fruit bearing:

1. *A person must be connected to the right source.*

In John 15:4-5 Jesus says, "Remain in me, and I will remain in you. No branch can bear fruit by itself; it must remain in the vine. Neither can you bear fruit unless you remain in me. I am the vine; you are the branches. If a man remains in me and I in him, he will bear much fruit; apart from me you can do nothing." Many people who are frustrat-

What a difference it makes to realize that to be connected to God means His power is our power!

ed by the lack of fruit in their lives have never had a right relationship with God. Their fruit is artificial and not satisfying. Their independent spirit has shriveled their resources until their production is limited to their small, cramped capacity to produce. What a difference it makes to realize that to be connected to God means *His* power is *our* power! What's His becomes ours. No longer is it a question of "How can I expand my potential?" but rather "How can I allow God's power to flow through me?"

2. *A person must be pruned and disciplined to be fruitful.*

Jesus said in John 15:2, "He cuts off every branch in me that bears no fruit, while every branch that does bear fruit he prunes so that it will be even more fruitful." Fruit bearing is God's highest desire for your life. He wants you to bear *more* fruit. He is the source of unlimited blessings that should flow from your life to others. He wants you to be disciplined in order to be the channel for greater fruitfulness. For this to become a reality, you must allow Him to remove every hindrance to fruit bearing in your life. You will be fruitful only as you become disciplined. Pruning is the price for production. My favorite pastime is reading about the lives of great men and women. As I study their lives, it's evident that the first victory they won was the victory over themselves.

3. *A person must realize that God's purpose for His children is fruitfulness.*

"This is to my Father's glory, that you bear much fruit, showing yourselves to be my disciples" (John 15:8). Once God's purpose is discovered, it's much easier to do His will. The fruit of the Spirit should be your key to effective fruit bearing. Keep your relationship right with God, keep your life disciplined, and with all your strength fulfill God's purpose for your life. Your constant contact with the Vine will make it possible.

PART II
POINTERS ON POTENTIAL

8

YES, YOU CAN!

One of my special joys in leading people is the privilege of helping them to believe in themselves. Regardless of their age, gender, or background, it's a challenge to help instill within an individual a self-confidence that will eliminate uncertainty about solving a problem and help him or her establish a positive outlook regarding the solution.

It's amazing how many people allow their thinking to determine how much they accomplish in life. Comments such as "It's never been done before," "Don't be a dreamer," and "Don't get your hopes up too much" have stymied the potential of many would-be achievers in life. Too many people are dwelling in slums when they should be rising to the stars.

One year in the fall my wife and I decided to take a drive through the hills of southern Ohio. It was a warm day, and just before we left town we decided to stop for a cold drink. We pulled into a fast-food restaurant to place the order, only to discover that this restaurant did not serve diet soft drinks, which is what my wife wanted. So I ordered a cola and a large cup of ice, thinking I would stop at a store and buy a can of diet pop for Margaret.

When I placed my order for the cola and a large cup of ice, the waitress said sadly, "I don't think I can do that."

I quickly reassured her by replying, "Yes, you can."

Her face lit up almost immediately as she said, "OK" and went hurrying off to fill my order. What she needed was someone to reassure her that she could do what was asked.

Very often people fail to get involved in working and helping others, not because they lack the ability or willingness to do so, but because they lack the confidence and assurance that they can do the job.

Very often people fail to get involved in working and helping others, not because they lack the ability or willingness to do so, but because they lack the confidence and assurance that they can do the job.

Many people see such a large problem in front of them that they're unable to comprehend the possibility of either overcoming or avoiding that particular obstacle. One day I pulled into a service station to fill my car with gas. While waiting, I noticed that a bus had blocked a lady into a parking lot. One look at her, and I could see she was totally frustrated and defeated. As I sized up the situation, it was evident to me that she could get out of the parking lot if she could simply be persuaded to try. She felt it was hopeless because all she could see was the big bus in front of her, keeping her from her goal of leaving the parking lot.

I instructed the friend who was traveling with me to go to her window, tell her to watch me, and I would direct her between the bus and the gate out onto the road. I also told my friend to keep encouraging the lady by telling her she could drive the car through that narrow space. And sure enough, she made it. As we watched, her face turned from defeat to delight. Why? Because she accomplished something that moments before she thought was impossible.

What big barriers frustrate you and cause you to believe that your goals are impossible and unreachable? What negative note causes discord in your dreams or causes them to go flat or turn sour? Whatever the problem, stop for just one moment and consider the following statement: *A successful person is one who takes the cold water dumped on his or her plans, heats it with enthusiasm, and manufactures the steam that helps him or her push ahead.*

Years ago a group of new engineers in the Lamp Division of General Electric were assigned the seemingly impossible task of frosting bulbs on the inside. No one believed it was really possible, and it was largely treated as a joke. Eventually, however, an undaunted newcomer named Marion Pipkin not only found a way to frost bulbs on the inside but also developed an etching acid that produced minutely rounded pits instead of sharp depressions. This discovery actually strengthened each bulb. Fortunately, no one had convinced Mr. Pipkin that it couldn't be done—*so he did it!*

As we travel along the road of life, many negative seeds are planted in our minds until we often stop short of what we can do for God, for others, and for ourselves.

Too often the reverse is true. As we travel along the road of life, many negative seeds are planted in our minds until we often stop short of what we can do for God, for others, and for ourselves. The next time you're expecting to stop short of a goal, remember that I'm saying to you, "Yes, you can!" And if that's not enough, remember what the apostle Paul is also saying to you in Phil. 4:13, "I can do everything through him who gives me strength."

9

YOU CAN BE BETTER THAN AVERAGE

Defining the word "average," someone said, "'Average' is the best of the worst and the worst of the best."

A lady came up to me after I had preached on success and asked me, "What's wrong with being average?"

I replied, "If you're not a Christian, nothing's wrong with being average. If you're a Christian, then you must not be content until you develop to the fullest extent the potential God has given you. In doing this, you'll bring glory to God and be lifted above the average."

I'm not saying that you'll be more intelligent or better looking because you've become a Christian. But your attitude toward life, your consecration in service, and your abundant love will lift you above the average person. Read carefully the following principles, which will enable you to be better than average.

1. To rise above the common plane of living you need *a little more determination* than the average person.

Great people are just ordinary people with an extraordinary amount of determination. When those around you quit and throw up their hands, grit your teeth and dig in a little deeper. Success is achieved and maintained by those who keep trying. Go ahead—admit it: Today you may not be what you want to be, hope to be, or dream of becoming, but the one key to achieving your dream is determining not to quit.

> *"A man is a hero not because he is braver than anyone else, but because he is brave for ten minutes longer."*

Ralph Waldo Emerson said, "A man is a hero not because he is braver than anyone else, but because he is brave for ten minutes longer." A track star who runs a long distance learns to depend upon his "second wind." He runs until he's weary and exhausted. But he doesn't stop there. The average runner decides to quit, but the track star knows that if he can endure a little more pain, he'll get this "second wind." Until a person has tried hard enough and long enough to get his "second wind," he'll never know how much he can accomplish. Remember: ability is 95 percent "stickability."

2. To rise above the common plane of living you need *a little more faith* than the average person.

This world is a place of sorrow, confusion, and hurts. The person with that extra faith in God, others, and himself or herself will certainly rise above the crowd. It was this type of faith that caught the attention of Jesus when He healed the lady with an incurable disease. Many were touching Him that day in the crowd. It was that extra faith of hers that made the difference. Today every person needs that faith, which will light any path, relieve any distress, bring joy out of sorrow, peace out of strife, and friendship out of enmity.

When you possess that faith, you'll be used of God to light the path of those who stumble, encourage the hearts of those who faint, relieve the load of those whose burdens are heavy, and plant a song in the heart of those who are sad. When you do these things, you're far above average.

3. To rise above the common plane of living, you need *a little more love* than the average person.

This world is full of lonely individuals. People are surrounded by people, yet often feel alone. They need to be loved. In our society love can mean many things. We sing about it, read about it, try to find it, but we're really unsure of what it is. Love has hands to help others. It has feet to hasten to the poor and needy. It has eyes to see the hurts of the world. It has lips to encourage those in despair.

In a foreign country an unconverted tourist happened to see an American nurse dressing an open, leprous wound. The sight was a shocking one—revolting to the eye and stomach. "I wouldn't do that for a million dollars," he said to the Christian nurse.

"Neither would I," she smiled.

What a million dollars wouldn't do, God's love for others in her heart did!

Remember—you'll never be "just average" if you're a Christian, because you possess more determination, faith, and love than the average person.

10

SEE IT LIKE IT COULD BE

I was in college in 1968 when United States Senator Robert Kennedy was assassinated. A famous line he had quoted from George Bernard Shaw made a profound impression upon me. It leaped out of the pages of the newspaper into my heart: "Some men see things as they are and say 'Why?' I dream of things that never were and say, 'Why not?'" That statement describes effective leadership.

Leaders in all areas of life have distinguishing characteristics. One characteristic common to all is vision. Proverbs 29:18 says, "Where there is no vision, the people perish" (KJV). It's only right, then, to conclude that where there *is* a vision, the people will *not* perish. Leaders see life as it could be. They are always seeing a little farther, a little more, than those around them.

The world says, "I have to see it to believe it." The leader says, "I have to believe it to see it."

The crowds shake their heads in despair and mutter, "This is humanity's darkest hour." The leader in the midst of darkness says, "The darkest hour is just before the dawn."

The loser sees the work that needs to be done and limply excuses himself by saying, "My little bit will make no difference—the task is too great." The winner looks at the same work that needs to be done and says, "Here's a great opportunity—I'll do my part to make it succeed."

Followers see the hard work they must endure in order to climb the mountain of success. Leaders see the success of climbing the mountain of hard work. Many people see the problem in every situation. Therefore, they center their thinking upon the problems and the possibility of failure. Leaders see the potential in every situation. Therefore, they concentrate their thinking upon the potential and the possibility of success.

Followers see the hard work they must endure in order to climb the mountain of success. Leaders see the success of climbing the mountain of hard work.

It's possible for two people to look at the same object and see different things. While our physical eyesight is very important, our mental eyesight is equally so. Why is it that we carefully schedule checkups of our physical vision but not our mental vision? The last time I visited my optometrist, he checked my eyes and stated that I was a little farsighted. I responded, "Praise the Lord!" If I was going to have eye problems, I concluded, farsightedness certainly was better than nearsightedness. The church has a large-enough supply of nearsighted people.

How is your mental eyesight? Give yourself the following checkup on how you see things.

1. When I hear a new idea the first time, do I see potential in that new thought?

(*a*) Most of the time. (*b*) Sometimes. (*c*) Few times.

2. Do I share new thoughts with others most of the time, or are others usually sharing new ideas with me?

(*a*) I share new ideas most of the time. (*b*) Sharing and receiving are about equal. (*c*) Others usually share ideas with me.

3. How do I think when I'm in a group and a new problem arises that requires a decision?

(*a*) I'll go along with the others. (*b*) I'm glad I don't have to make decisions. (*c*) I'm responsible to encourage others to make a responsible decision.

4. How do I generally view life?

(*a*) Difficult. (*b*) Challenging. (*c*) Good and bad, depending on situations.

5. How do I react when faced with responsibility?

(*a*) Accept it. (*b*) Pass it on. (*c*) Reject it.

If you're a leader and have mental farsightedness, your answers were probably (1) *a;* (2) *b;* (3) *a;* (4) *c;* (5) *b.* If you're mentally nearsighted, your answers probably were (1) *c;* (2) *c;* (3) *b;* (4) *a;* (5) *c.*

11

TELL IT LIKE IT COULD BE

When people are stressing honesty and wanting communication to be meaningful and effective, they'll often say, "Tell it like it is." Recent outbreaks of dishonesty, corruption, and cover-up in leadership positions have forced the public to cry out loudly, "Tell it like it is!" Preachers mount the pulpit on Sunday and with a holy enthusiasm begin to "tell it like it is." In heavy traffic, horns blow and fists shake, "telling it like it is." Even United States consumer advocate Ralph Nader says he "tells it like it is."

In the midst of a world that shouts, "Tell it like it is!" let me share a great motivational thought with you. The next time you want to help someone who's in difficulty, stop and think. Why not change your approach? Instead of "telling it like it is" why not "tell it like it could be"? Before you begin to question my motives, let me state that I'm not asking you to be dishonest. I didn't say, "Tell it like it could *never* be." I said, "Tell it like it *could* be"!

How many good things can happen when you "tell it like it *could* be"?

1. *You lift the problem-plagued person out of his or her present circumstances.*

Who doesn't need a lift in this world of letdowns? Who doesn't need a pull in this world of setbacks? Who doesn't need a pat on the back in a world that kicks us in the seat of the pants?

One of the prime responsibilities of a leader is to encourage others. Most of my dealing with people occurs in counseling sessions in my office. The reason is obvious. I desire to take them out of their environment, away from their problems, into an atmosphere that is pleasant, relaxing, and conducive to effective communication.

2. *You help the person see things more clearly.*

There's no better way to change a problem than to help someone see a solution. Many times people with problems become slaves to their situation because they can see nothing but problems. The saying "I can't see the forest for the trees" is applicable here. Help others see the potential in all their situations and circumstances.

Many times people with problems become slaves to their situation because they can see nothing but problems.

Many times individuals will sit in my office and begin a counseling session with these words: "I'm sure you've never had to deal with a problem like mine." They're depressed. Perhaps they're even taking the liberty to indulge in a little self-pity. They feel their problem is unique. Lift them out of their dungeon of depression and let them see the sunshine. Nothing will more quickly and effectively shrivel a bad situation into proper perspective than focusing attention upon the positive elements of a problem.

3. *You give the person a dream.*

Everyone needs a dream. Many good people with a lot of potential are going nowhere because they have no dream. Mac Davis says, "There's nothing to do but hang a man when he has no dreams." I'm convinced that some elderly people become depressed and die much earlier than necessary because they quit looking into the future with hope and expectation and begin looking back into the past with futility and frustration. A good dream is like cream—it will lift you to the top.

4. *You help the individual reach his or her potential.*

Every person has hidden potential. No one has ever become all he or she can become. No one will make important strides toward developing and fulfilling his or her potential until made to see the possibilities. Neither you, nor I, nor anyone else will ever be all that God intends for us to be until we focus in on what we can become.

5. *You give the person confidence.*

One of the first steps to solving problems is to establish confidence. The more confidence you can instill in another person, the greater the chance of his or her overcoming the barriers. When people have the same spirit as expressed by the apostle Paul—"I can do all things through him who gives me strength" (Phil. 4:13)—they're going to go over the top in all areas of life.

6. *You change the atmosphere in which people live.*

Low morale is lifted. Quality is upgraded. Possibilities are highlighted. Smiles are in abundance. Excitement is in the air. Thinking is positive. Ideas are creative. Problems are stepping-stones. Goals are set. Progress is made. Why? Because you *told it like it could be!*

12

THREE MISTAKES
TOO OFTEN MADE

The following mistakes, I believe, are the most commonly made:

1. *Believing that mistakes are always to be avoided.*

The reason people try to avoid mistakes is that they feel they are a sign of failure or weakness. But mistakes can become learning experiences. If you haven't made any mistakes lately, I question whether you're trying hard enough. Not all avenues have been pursued. Not all channels have been covered.

We learn from our mistakes. It probably can be said further that a person cannot learn without making them. Perhaps we would learn more from our mistakes if we were not so busy denying that we make them. Fear of making mistakes has kept many people from rising to the top.

During a church growth convention that I was conducting, a lady raised her hand and asked, "Do you ever fail when you go soul winning?"

I quickly replied, "No." She could not believe what she heard, so she repeated the question.

I gave the same reply. She jumped to her feet and said, "Do you mean to tell me that *every* time you witness, you win someone to Christ?"

I replied, "No, not everyone becomes a Christian."

"But you said you never failed when witnessing!" she exclaimed.

I tried to clarify the point by explaining that just because a person did not receive Christ when I witnessed to him or her did not mean I had made a mistake or had failed. All I was responsible to do was share Christ with the person. It's not my job to save him or her. The failure lies in being one who never shares his or her faith with others. Fear of rejection, mistakes, and failure causes people to make the worst mistake of all—that of *doing nothing*.

When you make a mistake, you can resolve never to make another one. But that's an impossible resolution. You can decide that mistakes are too costly and become fearful of them, but that fear will keep you from fulfilling your potential. You can constantly think about your mistakes and live with regret, but that's self-torture. Finally, you can learn from your mistakes and become a better person, and that's progress.

2. *Thinking that success comes naturally to those who are the most brilliant and talented.*

History has proven that people are successful not because of brilliance, but because of persistence and desire. A young man who was learning how to become a trapeze artist heard some excellent advice from his teacher, who said, "Throw your heart over the bars, and your body will follow." No matter what field of endeavor we're pursuing, those of us who throw our hearts into our work will know success.

> *History has proven that people are successful not because of brilliance, but because of persistence and desire.*

The degree of success you achieve depends upon the amount of sincere desire you possess. Successful people have a dream that becomes too exciting, too important to remain in the realm of fantasy. Their dream becomes a burning desire. Day by day, hour by hour, minute by minute, they toil in the service of their dreams until they can see it with their eyes and touch it with their hands.

The true measure of success is not what position you've reached in life, but what obstacles you have overcome to reach the desired goal.

Persistence is needed for one to be an achiever. Success is never instantaneous. It's never an accident. Success is continuous. It takes growth and development. It's achieving one thing and using that as a stepping-stone to rise higher up the mountain of accomplishment. The true measure of success is not what position you've reached in life, but what obstacles you have overcome to reach the desired goal. Obstacles are overcome by persistence.

3. *Refusing to change when there's a need to change.*

One of my favorite stories is about an old fellow who was coming up on his 100th birthday. A newspaper reporter went to interview him. Approaching the elderly gentleman politely, he said, "Sir, you must have seen a great many changes during your hundred years."

The old man gazed steadily at him for a moment, then replied, "Yes, and I've been agin all of 'em."

I'm afraid this man's attitude is the attitude of far too many other people as well.

It's so easy to sit in a rut and let the world pass us by after we've raised our objections to all changes. Perhaps we should take out our negative, closed mind every once in a while and stomp on it to get all the cogs out. What's truly sad about those who won't change is that there can be no improvement except through change. To keep changing is not an end in itself, but only through change can there be true growth.

People resist change because they're basically insecure. What if we fail? How do we deal with the unknown? A church board asked me what they should do to get their church growing. This church had been running about 30 in attendance for the past 30 years. I suggested a few changes that could help their situation.

Immediately the board responded by saying in essence, "We can't make those changes—we might fail."

I asked them if their lack of growth did not, right at the time, point to their failure. They were *already* failing! Change could not hurt them and could possibly be the vehicle toward growth.

People resist change because it takes energy to do something different. Exchanging ideas, planning, rearranging priorities, and setting new goals are activities that take time and effort. It's always easier to stay in the same rut, but it's not always right and best. Every growing organism grows to maturity, levels off, and dies unless there's new life, new blood, new activity, and new ideas. In other words, we die unless we continue to grow. We grow only when we change.

13

FALL DOWN NINE TIMES— GET UP TEN

Our daughter, Sara Elizabeth, was about to celebrate her first birthday. She had started making a few feeble attempts to walk. My wife, Margaret, and I enjoyed sitting on the floor across from each other, encouraging Sara Elizabeth to take a few wobbly steps. When she successfully completed her walk, we clapped and cheered. If she began to fall, we tried to catch her. If she did fall, we encouraged her to get back up.

Life is very much like a baby who is just learning to walk. There are days in which the going is smooth. Success is ours to enjoy. But there are also days of distress, hours of hindrance, minutes of misunderstandings, and seconds of stumbling. Since the path of life is rocky, and the road toward the top has many unexpected turns, it is important for you to realize three things concerning the "potholes" on the road to the top.

1. *There will be times when you fall.*

Anyone who walks down the path of life not only has the privilege of enjoying it but also must take the risk of falling. When you rise to the occasion you may fall prey to the enemy. Any person that is willing to stand for some-

The more we attempt to do, the more likelihood that we'll fall.

thing may at times be knocked down. We sometimes, like Sara Elizabeth, become careless and get in a hurry. Many times this happens just before we meet our goal. It looks as though we've been successful. The obstacles have been overcome. The sweet smell of victory permeates the air. But then . . .

A few years ago I watched a football player make an exciting run through the defensive line and with skill and speed outrun the defensive backs. Just as he was approaching the goal line, he thrust his hands into the air, and the football popped out of his hands. He fumbled on the three-yard line. I'll never forget the look of surprise and disappointment that came over his face. I, too, have sometimes been careless and fallen down just before reaching the goal. I can very definitely relate to his feelings.

Sometimes our inexperience causes us to fall. Sometimes lack of preparation is the problem. Maybe the problem is overconfidence. One thing is certain: Regardless of the reason for falling, we all at times trip—and *down* we fall.

2. *The more we attempt to do, the more likelihood that we'll fall.*

My mother tells me that when I was about one year old, I began to walk. As I attempted to do various maneuvers while walking, suddenly I had a terrible fall and did not try to walk again until I was 16 months old. My problem was that as a baby I allowed the shock of that fall to control my actions instead of being controlled by the success of accomplishment.

3. *The difference between success and failure is how we react after the fall.*

If we become involved with life and become players instead of spectators, the obstacles of life will sometimes trip us. The lives of many people have gone awry because of mistakes they made or bad experiences that came their way. They have allowed the bitter taste of defeat to remain in their mouths until only notes of negativism spill out. Their lives have been centered around the fall instead of the excitement of their journey.

The Bible gives a classic example of how reacting to a fall determines our outcome. King Saul and King David both sat on the throne of Israel. Both were chosen of God and had many talents. Both fell. King Saul allowed his mistake to harden his heart, and he died a violent death. King David repented and asked God's forgiveness and had fruitful years of leadership after his sin.

Remember: the failure is *not* in the fall. The failure is in allowing our fall to keep us down and to control our lives. Determine to be like a college classmate of mine who stood up in chapel and said, "I'm never down. I'm either up or getting up."

14

AN EAGLE DOESN'T ROOST IN A SPARROW'S NEST

It's 4 A.M., and I can't get those words of famous English preacher Joseph Parker out of my mind: "An eagle does not roost in a sparrow's nest." The Bible also has something to say about the sparrow and the eagle. Jesus illustrated the care of our Heavenly Father by saying that even when a common sparrow falls, God notices. The sparrow represents something rather insignificant and of lesser value. The eagle, in contrast to the sparrow, is pictured as strong and great as it soars into the high heavens.

One of my favorite passages of Scripture is Isa. 40:28-31: "Do you not know? Have you not heard? The LORD is the everlasting God, the Creator of the ends of the earth. He will not grow tired or weary, and his understanding no one can fathom. He gives strength to the weary and increases the power of the weak. Even youths grow tired and weary, and young men stumble and fall; but those who hope in the LORD will renew their strength. They will soar on wings like eagles; they will run and not grow weary, they will walk and not be faint." What a thrill to know that there's a power from God that will help us attain *spiritual* heights as the eagle attains physical heights!

You and I as born-again believers ought to be like the eagle, never content to roost in a sparrow's nest. God has designed and empowered us to be like the eagle. Each day it's possible to reach another unknown height. Moment by moment, experiences of growth and adventure in walking by faith can be ours. Yet it's evident that many Christians have settled into a sparrow's nest.

Some people become more satisfied with their positions than their growth.

The reason for this level of living, though sad, is obvious. Some people become more satisfied with their positions than their growth. There are certain levels of nesting upon the mountain of life that appealingly say, "Stop here, settle down, and be satisfied."

There's a mountain near my former home of Lancaster, Ohio, that I used to climb quite often. Along the path up the mountain are many resting places. Often people will stop to rest and renew their strength before continuing their walk to the summit.

I used to watch with great interest as climbers would look up toward the top of the mountain and then decide to climb no higher. They felt content to sit and wait while their friends continued to climb. Instead of stopping for renewal, they decided to stay and camp. Instead of receiving strength to go higher, they rested on what they have achieved and settled into the "sparrow's nest."

We, too, can choose to be numbered with the many who have decided that the price is too great, the sacrifice too demanding, and the benefits of climbing too small. We can choose to sit. We can watch others climb. There will be an offer of a seat for anyone who is tired, plus sympathy and 17 reasons why it is not necessary to climb higher. Words of discouragement are contagious. Soon we could be sitting around the "sparrow's nest."

It's easier to talk about climbing than to climb. It's easier to "chew the fat" than to walk it off. The mountain is so much like real life. There are more at the bottom than at the top. The "sparrow's nest" is a popular place.

But there are always those in life who are like the eagles. We can choose to keep our eyes on the heights. Slowly, steadily, with determination, we can pass the "sparrow's nest." We need not be distracted by the living monuments of quitters who mark the pathway to the top of the mountain. Each one who has settled for a second best is a reminder to us that life is a journey and not a destination, that joy comes through striving and not through settling down, that victory and quitting are not compatible.

> *We need not be distracted by the living monuments of quitters who mark the pathway to the top of the mountain.*

We can climb onward and upward like the eagle. Those perched in the sparrow's nest look on with great interest. The moment the climbers hesitate, the quitters will encourage them to stop. If we continue to climb, they will criticize. If we achieve, they will rationalize.

Finally, we arrive at the top. It is less crowded now, but the caliber of those who make it is different. At the summit you will find those who are encouragers. We find great fellowship and conversation about discipline, sacrifice, joy, happiness, achievement, and success. No hard-luck stories on top of the mountain. No critical, envious, and bitter spirits. No bad attitudes or chips on shoulders. No sour dispositions or negative thinking. It is so *good* to be on top of the mountain. The air is clear. The vision is great. The beauty is something to behold. The fellowship is wonderful, and the feeling is good.

But that feeling of satisfaction comes only after victory. That feeling is the result of hard work and determination. That feeling of exhilaration surges through you when you know you've done everything possible to fulfill the potential God has given you. That feeling of achievement assures you that your talents and energies have been wisely expended. You have soared like the eagle. You have seen too much to be satisfied with less! You have experienced too many exciting adventures to settle for second best. Yes, you have climbed like the eagle, and there's nothing that can make you roost in the sparrow's nest again—ever.

15

YOU AND I CAN CHANGE OUR WORLD

I love the story about the 10-year-old boy who was selling pencils door to door in his neighborhood. When an interested adult at one house asked him the reason for selling pencils, he replied, "I want to raise six million dollars to build a new hospital for the city."

Amazed, the inquiring adult exclaimed, "That's a mighty big job for just one little boy, isn't it?"

"No," responded the 10-year-old with big dreams. "I have a friend who's helping me."

The world God created is a big, beautiful place in which to live. But the world that humanity has ruined needs to be changed. Yet, it is so large and complex that I don't think I can change it by myself. I need your help! Just you? That's right—just you. We must change with the times unless we are big enough to change the times. George Bernard Shaw said, "The reasonable man adapts himself to the world; the unreasonable man attempts to adapt the world to himself. Therefore, all progress depends on the unreasonable man." If you and I are willing to be unreasonable, perhaps we can change our world. You see, history has been altered in times past by various groups of people. Here are some examples.

History was changed . . .

> *If you and I are willing to be unreasonable, perhaps we can change our world.*

By 50,000. King David had an army of "fifty thousand, which could keep rank: they were not of double heart" (1 Chron. 12:33, KJV). If 50,000 cannot be found, what then? It was changed . . .

By 7,000. God told Elijah that there were "seven thousand in Israel—all whose knees have not bowed down to Baal" (1 Kings 19:18). Certainly God has 7,000 as there were in Elijah's day to stand for Him! But if not, our world can still be changed. It *was* changed . . .

By 300. Just a small portion of Gideon's original army was needed by God for victory. Judges 7:7 tells of the Lord's promise that "with the three hundred men that lapped I will save you and give the Midianites into your hands." But if 300 cannot be found, the world can still be changed. It *was* changed . . .

By 120. Those who were willing to pay the price of waiting on God and were "with one accord in one place" (Acts 2:1, KJV) until "they were all filled with the Holy Ghost" (4:31, KJV). Yet in this day of shallowness and luke-warmness, though there perhaps are not even 120, thank God—it can still be changed. It *was* changed . . .

By 50. Robert E. Speer said around 1917, "If fifty men in our congregation can be found who will enter the holy place of prayer and become henceforth men whose hearts God has touched with prayer passion, the history of the church will be changed." But if 50 cannot be found, our world can still be changed. It *was* changed . . .

By 10. Dwight L. Moody said, "If ten men will give themselves completely to the will of God, they will be able to change the world." God said to Abraham, "For the sake of ten, I will not destroy it" (Gen. 18:32). But even if there are not 10 completely sold out to the will of God, this world can still be changed . . .

By two. Jesus said in Matt. 18:19-20, "I tell you that if two of you on earth agree about anything you ask for, it will be done for you by my Father in heaven. For where two or three come together in my name, there am I with them." You see, two people can change the world. Will you join with me? God needs both of us and wants to use us, because you and I *can* change our world!

16

THE GREATEST SIN
IN THE WORLD

What's the greatest sin? Lying? Cheating? Adultery? Stealing? Cursing? No. These are all sins, but not the worst one. Adam committed the greatest sin in the world, and so have all his descendants. Adam failed to become all that his Creator, God, intended him to be. A perfect relationship between God and humanity became imperfect. A life of discovery became a life of drudgery. Beauty was replaced with ashes. Serenity was washed away by sweat. Thorns and weeds displaced flowers as sin placed its mark upon humanity. Why? Because Adam failed to become all that God intended him to be.

The greatest waste of energy in our world is not that of electricity or fuel. The greatest energy shortage today is the unused potential within the lives of people. How about you? It's stated that the average person uses only about 10 percent of his or her potential. What would happen if each one of us could raise his or her potential level from 10 percent to 25 percent?

Let me share with you a positive, three-step procedure that will enable you to become more the person God desires you to be.

Step One: *Discover your potential.* I love the story about a young farm boy whose father raised chickens in the mountains of Colorado. One day this adventuresome boy climbed to a high place in the mountains and found an eagle's nest. He took an egg out of the nest, brought it back to the farm, and put it under a setting hen.

The hen didn't know the difference—an egg was an egg to her. Her only instinct was to sit on her eggs until they hatched. So out came a little eaglet with the chickens, and they all lived a "chicken's life" together. The eaglet thought he was a chicken. He didn't have a mirror to look into to see that he looked different. And for the time being, he was content to be with the chickens.

When you're content with a small crowd, you remain small yourself. If you live with critical people, you become critical. If you associate with negative, defeated people, then likely you will be negative and defeated also. You're "living with the chickens."

But as the eaglet grew, he felt strange stirrings within himself. Every once in a while he would think, "There's more to me than a chicken." But he never did anything about it until one day an eagle flew over the chicken yard, and the little eaglet said, "I'm like that eagle."

The eaglet felt the strength in his wings and thought, "This narrow chicken yard is not for me. I want to see the sky and the mountain peaks!" He had never flown, but the power and the instinct were there within him, and he soared to the top of a high hill and then on into the blue, where he landed on a high mountain crag. He had discovered that he could fly!

One of the greatest days of your life will be the day when you discover your potential.

One of the greatest days of your life will be the day when you discover your potential. You and your talents are not an accident. You're not a number in a lineup. You're not a statistic lost in the shuffle of mass humanity. You are special in God's eyes. You have distinct gifts and talents. You have shoes to fill that no one else can wear. Inside you is enormous potential just waiting to be developed and put to use.

Step Two: *Dedicate your potential.* Give to God all you are and all you have. It makes good common sense. Since God created you for a purpose, it's only with God that you can become what He intends. The apostle Paul recognized this when he said, "I can do everything through him who gives me strength" (Phil. 4:13).

Step Three: *Develop your potential.* God's gift to you is your potential. What you do with it is your gift to God. God is concerned not only about what you are but also about what you can become. In order to develop your potential to its fullest capacity, it will be necessary to implement the following items into your daily life:

If you believe that you have little to offer the world, you'll sit and contribute nothing.

a. Develop a positive self-image. It's no accident that as your self-image changes, your performance changes. Your actions are a direct result of how you see yourself. Those who think little of themselves produce little. A person who pictures himself or herself as a failure will be a failure. If you believe that you have little to offer the world, you'll sit and contribute nothing. But when you begin to feel good about yourself, you'll begin to feel good toward others. As you feel worthwhile, you'll become worthwhile. The better your self-image becomes, the greater the development of your potential.

*b. Realize that **you** are responsible for developing your potential.* It's important to realize that God judges you not nearly as much on what you are as on what you can become. The Bible says, "From everyone who has been given much, much will be demanded" (Luke 12:48).

c. Realize that God is more interested in having you develop your potential than He is concerned about the mistakes you make. For too long individual churches have nitpicked people who have tried and failed. Therefore, the potential of these churches has never been realized because they major on shortcomings. God does not have a club in His hand waiting to beat down your desire to live an effective life. He has His hand outstretched to help you develop your life to its most fruitful capacity.

d. Get acquainted with others who are successful in developing their abilities. It's not by chance that winners spend time together. It's a well-known fact that after Roger Bannister broke the four-minute mile, which most people thought could never be done, within 10 years 336 other men had accomplished that same feat. Why? Because they were exposed to someone who exhib-

> *It's interesting to note that the 1936 Olympics records were the qualifying standards for the 1972 Olympics.*

ited more potential than what many felt they had. One of

Jack Nicklaus's goals was to win more major tournaments than any other man in the history of golf. When a reporter asked him if he ever felt his record would be broken, he replied quickly, "Oh, yes—all records will be broken sometime by someone." Why? Because men and women are always expanding their potential. It's interesting to note that the 1936 Olympics records were the qualifying standards for the 1972 Olympics.

What's your capacity? That's really hard to predict. Over 50 years ago Johnny Weissmuller was called the greatest swimmer the world had ever known. Doctors and coaches around the world said nobody would ever break his records. He held over 50 of them. Do you know who's breaking "Tarzan's" records today? Thirteen-year-olds!

Let me challenge you. Get on your knees and ask God to forgive you for failing to be at your best. Then get up and discover your potential. Dedicate it to God, and develop it by changing your self-image. Realize your responsibility, acknowledge God's interest in you, and acquaint yourself with others who have been successful in developing themselves. Now go out and break a record!

PART III
STATEMENTS ON SUCCESS

17

WHAT IS SUCCESS?

This is a day when we hear much about success. Books are written almost every day concerning this subject. Clinics, seminars, and rallies motivating others to successful living can be found in almost every city. We read about it, hear about it, and work hard to achieve it. But what *is* success?

When I consented to God's call to preach the gospel, I began to save illustrations, quotes, poems, and any other information that I would someday find valuable for speaking. Over the years I have accumulated a great amount of material concerning various subjects. Especially under the heading of "success" I have gathered many informative thoughts, including the secrets, stories, rules, ingredients, formulas, guidelines, philosophies, measures, keys, science, traits, plans, and steps of success. After spending time studying the subject and mingling with all types of people, allow me to share with you my definition.

> *"Success is choosing to enter the arena of action, determined to give yourself to the cause that will better humanity and last for eternity."*

"Success is choosing to enter the arena of action, determined to give yourself to the cause that will better humanity and last for eternity." Included in this definition of success are seven vital ingredients.

1. Success is *choosing.*

Since it involves a decision, success is knowing a truth and accepting it! Our society is full of plastic buildings on the foundation of false hopes. We live in a day of shortcuts, loopholes, and "one more for the road," as we look for an exit to escape reality. We're not successful until we know what's right and then do it.

2. Success is choosing to enter the arena of *action*.

Success is finding a need and filling it. Many people can find a need, point to the problem, and size up the situation. Only a successful person goes that next step beyond finding the need—he or she endeavors to fill it.

The story of the Good Samaritan vividly illustrates the difference between a winner and a loser. A man was robbed, beaten, and left to die alongside the road. A priest saw the need and passed him by. A Levite saw the need and went on without helping. But the Good Samaritan not only saw the need but endeavored to meet it. He was not content to be a spectator.

The way to the top is not "stepping on others" but "stooping to help others."

Every person who has felt responsible to help someone else will quickly agree with the following truth: "No person can sincerely try to help another person without helping himself or herself." In other words, "You can get everything in life you want, if you help enough other people get what they want," Zig Ziglar declares. The way to the top is not "stepping on others" but "stooping to help others."

3. Success is choosing to enter the arena of action *determined.*

Success is facing a challenge and meeting it. Once you enter into the arena of action, be ready for problems. Little problems that nibble. Big problems that devour. Nagging problems that persist. Perplexing problems that confuse. Problems come in all sizes and shapes. They come at all times. Like death, problems are not respecters of persons.

Problems are the great dividers between success and failure. How you handle them will determine on which side you'll live.

It's not nearly as important where you're located when problems come as where you are when the problems are over. No problem will leave you the same person after it has gone. Problems are the great dividers between success and failure. How you handle them will determine on which side you'll live.

4. Success is choosing to enter the arena of action determined to *give yourself.*

Success is losing a life and finding it. Jesus said, "Whoever finds his life will lose it, and whoever loses his life for my sake will find it." What you keep you lose and what you lose you keep! What a paradox! One of the reasons many have never tasted sweet success is that they're unwilling to sacrifice to achieve. Life is a just bargainer. You give little, and you receive little. You give much, and you receive more.

I always enjoy watching the Olympics. The pomp of the program, the strategy of the teams, the support of the fans, the international interest, the grace and skill of the athletes, and the ecstasy of victory all bring me enjoyment. However, my greatest thrill is seeing the dedication of those athletes. Years of training, days of discouragement, periods of pain—all play a part in the lives of the athletes as they prepare for the competition. More gold medals have been won because of consecration and sacrifice than by natural abilities and "lucky breaks." A person never truly lives until he or she has a reason to die for something.

5. Success is choosing to enter the arena of action determined to give yourself to *that cause.*

Success is having a plan and following it. The apostle Paul said, "We are God's workmanship, created in Christ Jesus to do good works, which God prepared in advance for us to do" (Eph. 2:10). God has created you for a purpose. It's easy to see what an individual is pursuing in his or her goals for life. The way the person undertakes his or her affairs is largely determined by the way the person sees his or her goals. Are you excited as you pursue the goals that you and God have set?

6. Success is choosing to enter the arena of action determined to give yourself to the cause that will *better humanity*.

Success is developing a talent and sharing it, not merely having talents. Nothing is more distressing than seeing people with great ability sitting on the shelf of life. When we

> *Nothing is more distressing than seeing people with great ability sitting on the shelf of life.*

study the parable of the talents, it's evident that those who share and invest their talents, regardless of the number, increase and develop them.

Several years ago I thought it would be nice if one of the men who shared and invested his talents in Jesus' parable had lost one or more of them. I thought that would prove he was human. But the more I have studied the parable of the talents and observed those people who have lived lives of giving to others, the more I have come to the conclusion that it's impossible to lose what you share with others.

7. Success is choosing to enter the arena of action determined to give yourself to the cause that will better humanity and *last for eternity*.

Success is going to heaven and knowing it! As a child growing up in a Christian home, I remember well a plaque on the wall of our home that had the following words inscribed on it:

> *Only one life*
>   *'Twill soon be past.*
> *Only what's done*
>   *For Christ will last.*

> Success is
> *Knowing a truth and accepting it;*
> *Finding a need and filling it;*
> *Facing a challenge and meeting it;*
> *Losing a life and finding it;*
> *Having a plan and following it;*
> *Developing a talent and sharing it;*
> *Going to heaven and knowing it.*

I wish you all the success in the world!

18

COMMITMENT IS THE KEY

W. H. Murray wrote some lines that speak impressively of commitment: "Concerning all acts of initiative (and creation), there is one elementary truth the ignorance of which kills countless ideas and splendid plans: that the moment one definitely commits oneself, the providence moves too. A whole stream of events issues from the decision, raising in one's favor all manner of unforeseen incidents, meetings and material assistance, which no man could have dreamt would have come his way."

History is full of people who were advised to quit just short of a great accomplishment. Experts told Benjamin Franklin to leave alone all that foolish experimenting with lightning, that it was a waste of time. Fortunately, Franklin did *not* quit. He was committed!

Christopher Columbus had to face an impressive panel of experts, headed by Spain's leading geographer and scholar, who examined his plans and presented their findings to the king and queen of Portugal. They wrote, "Columbus's plan cannot be accomplished. Quite impossible." Christopher Columbus did not quit. He was committed!

Orville and Wilbur Wright were spending time and energy on a contraption that hopefully would fly into the air. Finally, in 1908, near Kitty Hawk, North Carolina, the Wright brothers taxied their crackpot idea down a sandy runway and launched the human race into the air. Orville and Wilbur Wright would not quit. They were committed!

Thomas Edison performed nearly 1,000 experiments before discovering the proper material for filament in the lightbulb. Edison would not quit. He was committed!

Edison urged Henry Ford to abandon his work on the fledgling idea of a motor car. "It's a worthless idea," remarked Edison.

However, Edison urged Henry Ford to abandon his work

on the fledgling idea of a motor car. "It's a worthless idea," remarked Edison. Ford would not quit. He was committed!

Experts told Madame Curie to forget her experimentation with radium. It was a scientific dead end. But she would not quit. She was committed!

Abraham Lincoln ran for the state legislature and failed. He entered business and failed, spending 17 years paying off his debts. He ran for Congress and was defeated. He ran for the United States Senate and lost. He finally became President of the United States. Lincoln would not quit. He was committed!

The key that unlocks the door to success is the key of commitment. Without that key, the door will never open. No amount of genius, talent, finesse, or "right connections" will ever bring the fruit of success without a real commitment. Most frustrated quitters never achieve their potential, not because of bad breaks or unusual problems, but because of a failure to commit themselves to their goal *regardless of obstacles.*

The level of your determination to accomplish your work is measured by what it takes to make you quit. Any reservation in your mind concerning the rightness of your plan will become a roadblock to you. Every great endeavor has a price tag. The greater the job, the higher the price.

That price tag is known as commitment. Take time to think about the following observations concerning commitment:

1. Lasting commitment is making the decision before the solution is found, knowing that the principle is right.

2. Commitment is the motivator that keeps a person moving toward his or her goal.

3. Commitment lets other people know where you stand and lets your heart feel the thrill of pursuing your objective.

4. Commitment gets you started while others stand, and keeps you going while others quit. *Commitment is the key!*

19

YOUR DECISIONS DETERMINE YOUR DESTINY

The importance of making proper decisions in life is illustrated in the lives of the children of Israel at Kadesh-barnea. As they came to the point that called for a decision, they began to waver. The following factors influenced them into making the wrong decision and paying a heavy price for their mistake:

1. Their *circumstances* caused the Israelites to make the wrong decision.

Walled cities and giants gave God's people the "grass-hopper" complex. They felt small, insignificant, powerless, and frustrated. Why? Because they looked at God in the light of their circumstances instead of the possibilities. They were more influenced by the size of men than by the size of God. The Jordan River wasn't the great barrier that kept them from Canaan. The hindrances that shattered them were beyond the Jordan.

They made the drastic mistake of trying to handle tomorrow's problems along with those of today. It was not today's difficulty that influenced their wrong decision, but tomorrow's anticipated problems that brought about their defeat. How true this is in our lives also! How many times has a wrong decision been the result of bringing tomorrow's imagined difficulties into today's situation? The load becomes staggering. Negative responses begin to spring up completely out of proportion. Panic sets in, and wrong decisions are made—decisions that determine our destiny.

2. The *negative influence* of the 10 spies kept God's children from experiencing His best for their lives

—10 men who said, "It can't be done"; 10 men who said, "We're just being realistic—we know the facts!"

Ten men kept thousands of people from finding God's perfect will for them. Ten men were more of an obstacle to the children of Israel than 10 walled cities the size of Jericho.

The enemies of God's people were not the Hittites, the Amalekites, or the Jebusites. God's enemies were *10 men* who said, "We can't do it; there's no way to victory." What stopped the Israelites from Canaan? Pharaoh's hard heart? The Red Sea? No food in the wilderness? The Jordan River? The walls of Jericho? Absolutely not! Just *10 men* who had an influence and used that influence in the wrong way.

It doesn't take a great multitude of people to limit God.

It doesn't take a great multitude of people to limit God. Just one unsurrendered Christian can be the doom of thousands without Christ. An unforgiving member can freeze out a revival. A couple of board members without faith and vision can hinder a great work that God wants to bring to a particular church. Ten negative men caused thousands to weep and stop short of God's promised blessings.

3. **Their *unwillingness to pay the price* was another factor that caused the Israelites to make the wrong decision.**

In every great endeavor, a price must be paid. The

greater the cause, the greater the cost. Men and women who have accomplished much have sacrificed much. Churches that have grown are churches that have groaned. Nothing given—nothing received. No weeping—no reaping.

No doubt the price to be paid for entering Canaan weighed heavily on every person's mind. If they went on into Canaan, their security would be threatened. They made the same mistake regarding security that some of us make today. They thought security was not having to confront the battles of life. The only security for the believer is not found in avoiding battles, temptations, and problems, but in *being found in the perfect will of God.* The children of Israel would have been more secure fighting giants in Canaan than wandering in the wilderness.

It was time for the Israelites to grow up and pay the sacrifice for victory as if victory depended upon them but relying upon God as if He alone could bring the victory. Up until this time God had supplied many miracles without asking His children to pay a price. Now the situation would have to change. Victory required two essentials—the work of God's children and the miracles of their God. The cities of Jordan would be conquered only when the soles of the feet of the people touched their territory. The walls of Jericho would fall only after God's children marched. For every blessing there was a price to be paid.

The children of Israel looked at their circumstances. They were influenced by 10 negative men who majored upon the problems. They decided they were not able to pay the price. So they made their decision—they chose to stay in the wilderness. For 40 years they wandered, getting nowhere, accomplishing nothing, living on God's second best. No new land. No milk and honey. No shouts of victory. Just wandering! Every person over 20 at the time, with the exception of Joshua and Caleb, never entered Canaan. They all died in the wilderness. They tried to save their lives, but they lost them.

Our decisions determine our destiny.

20

PLAN AHEAD

An old carpenter gave this advice to his young, inexperienced understudy: "Measure twice and saw once." That advice is worth heeding whether building houses or building lives. The plans established for any endeavor will greatly determine the end result.

Many years ago during a time of speaking to a group of leaders on this important subject of planning ahead, I developed a guideline to planning that has helped shape my life. Hopefully this simple formula will be of help to you as well.

1. *Predetermine a course of action.*

You'll never reach your goals until you discover the vehicle and direction needed to get you there. It seems strange that people will use a road map to guide them to a geographical location yet not feel the need to decide ahead of time what avenues they should travel to become a success in life. Just as road signs and mileage markers are indicators of progress made toward a geographical goal, so is the need for preplanned activity to help each person arrive successfully in all areas of life.

2. *Lay out your goals.*

The human scene is crowded with the people who have gone as far as they can go simply because they have nothing more to shoot for. James P. Cornette wrote, "One of the tragedies in life is for a man to arrive at the time when he has finished his tent and has nothing to do except play in it, with no new tent to begin."

3. *Adjust your priorities.*

Once your goals are set, there will be some rearranging of your priorities. Well-defined goals very quickly expose activities that are hindering progress toward certain objectives. Too often people tend to major on minors and to minor on majors.

4. *Notify your key personnel.*

Any great endeavor will take energy. People will supply energy. It's very important to communicate and receive positive feedback from those who are needed to help you reach the goal. Those who are informed and have opportunity to give positive feedback will help carry the ball toward the goal.

5. *Allow time for acceptance.*

Any new idea takes time before it can be fully endorsed. Proper presentation of ideas allows time for questions and consideration. Forcing change upon people is about as popular as German measles in an English army camp. Most people are more comfortable with old problems than with new solutions. A famous inventor said, "The world hates change, yet it is the only thing that has brought progress." Giving people sufficient time is the best way to have people accept change.

Most people are more comfortable with old problems than with new solutions.

6. *Head into action.*

After sufficient time is given to adopt new ideas, get going! Remember—nothing will ever be accomplished if you wait for everyone's approval or for the plan to be perfect. I love the story about General Douglas MacArthur during

World War II. He called one of his engineers and asked, "How long will it take to throw a bridge across the river?"

"Three days," the engineer replied.

"Good," snapped MacArthur. "Have your draftsmen make drawings right away."

Three days later the general sent for the engineer and asked how the bridge was coming along. "It's all ready," reported the engineer. "You can send your troops across right now if you don't have to wait for the plans. They ain't done yet."

7. *Expect problems.*

No plan eliminates all problems. Excellent planning will remove some obstacles, but not all of them. Problems are a part of life, and they'll appear to all of us. Change and progress will draw more opposition than deadness and stagnation. New challenges will arise. New questions will be asked. New solutions must be sought. Change affects emotions, and logic seldom wins in the arena of emotionalism. The barrier of ignorance must be crossed. The walls of insecurity must be climbed. The ceilings of the unimaginative must be lifted.

8. *Always point to the success of an endeavor.*

This is a great motivational tool when building for tomorrow. Sure, there will be mistakes and fumbles, but don't worry—someone will always be around to point to the problems. Nothing builds confidence like pointing to yesterday's victories. Nothing gives strength like knowing that what was done yesterday can be accomplished again today.

9. *Daily review your planning.*

The longer the projection, the greater the variation. Check daily to make sure you're still on target. If not, make the needed adjustments, and continue on toward success. A quick review is important to help us plan ahead.

21

SEVEN DETERMINANTS FOR VICTORY

March 19, 1978, was one of the great days of my life. Another goal was achieved—a milestone reached. A new victory was experienced: over 2,000 people attended the morning service at Faith Memorial Church! As I sat on the platform, I saw hundreds of happy, excited faces of people who were excited about this great victory, happy because the results were evident. The evening service was a time of rejoicing over what had been accomplished. Hearts were thrilled as one person after another stood to relate a success story about the morning service. A husband was saved. A family was brought back together. Still another family had attended church for the first time. In fact, over 200 people had attended our church that morning for the very first time.

Once the excitement was over, it was my joy to analyze and relish the victory. From this time of reflection came seven determinants for victory.

1. *A victory begins with a vision.*

A vision of winning—a vision of going "over the top." After the success, anyone can become inspired. It's easy after the victory to become excited with what has been accomplished. It takes no genius, determination, or extra ability to jump into the winner's circle after the game. The people who constantly rise to the top are those who possess a vision *before* the prize is won. They see the triumph before anyone else. During times of discouragement, they pursue the dream. While others criticize, they continue striving. They push aside the problems and point to the potential. They behave like victors before the contest. Why? Because they've already seen the victory in their mind.

2. *The next key to victory is instruction.*

Any achievement must be preceded by careful planning. The better we understand the problems, the greater our chance of victory. If we possess a knowledge of the tools at our disposal, we will more likely use them successfully.

3. *There is no success without proper conditioning.*

Sometimes victory is not achieved by the one who first

took the lead. The winner is the one who can work harder for longer periods of time *without quitting*. Many times the only difference between first and second place is the stamina and determination of the participants. I recall the endless running, jumping, squatting, and turning we used to endure during basketball practice sessions. The coach realized that skill without conditioning would be useless in the last

_____

The winner is the one who can work harder for longer periods of time without quitting.

_____

crucial minutes of the game. It would be interesting to know how many people stopped short of their goal because they were weary, and while resting became satisfied with their position.

4. *Victory can be realized only when one has a target.*

The thrill of victory comes only when a stated objective has been reached. No target, no thrill! No expectation, no exhilaration! How sad the plight of those individuals who will not let their desires be known for fear of failure! There are those who do not want to climb out on a limb for the fruit that is out there. No risk, no fruit! There must be a measure with which we can check our progress. Without a stated goal, we have no way of learning from our shortcomings. If we don't know where we're going, how do we know when we arrive? What's a football field without a goal line, a basketball game without a rim, and a baseball field without home plate?

5. *Victory can be secured only with the help of others.*

The greatest blessing received from our 2,000-plus attendance at Faith Memorial that Sunday was the assistance of many "others." No *one* person brought the crowd. It was many people willing to park their cars across the street in a nursing home parking lot so that visitors could have the best parking spots. It was others who called their friends, picked up their neighbors, and filled their cars. Victory doesn't say, "Look what *I* did," but "Look what *we* did." It's not *my* strength, but *our* strength; not *my* plans, but *our* plans; not *my* work, but *our* work. Therefore, it's not *my* victory, but *our* victory!

6. *Each person must fulfill his or her responsibility.*

Every person is important. Failure occurs when a person feels that if he or she does not work, it won't matter or won't hurt the group. God gives various gifts and abilities within the Church that we might do our job for total success.

7. *The last and most important key to victory is* you.

Only *you* have the power to determine the sacrifice, energy, and time that *you* will supply to become a winner.

Sometimes a person filled with self-pity will murmur that life has no options for him or her. That's never true. One thing worse than not having life options open to you is having open opportunities and not taking advantage of them. You're the only person who can determine to seize the opportunities of the moment. Victory or defeat—which will it be? Only *you* can answer that question. Remember: the seven determinants of VICTORY are **V**ision, **I**nstruction, **C**onditioning, **T**arget, **O**thers, **R**esponsibilities, and **Y**ou!

22

DISAPPOINTMENTS ARE NOT DEAD ENDS

Life is like a roller coaster—it has many ups and downs! There are times when the unexpected erupts, and our plans are abruptly changed. It's interesting to observe how people cope with the unexpected, especially if the sudden change has a negative bearing on their plans. We have all had our share of disappointments. We have all known what it means to have it rain on our parade. Our fondest hopes have sometimes been crushed.

The week I wrote this chapter 20 years ago was one of the most disappointing weeks of my life. Margaret, my wife, and I had been waiting for many months to adopt a baby girl. Finally, after endless delays and ups and downs, the final hearing in court was scheduled, and Sara Elizabeth was to be ours this week. The crib was painted, the curtains hung, and a new mattress purchased for the crib. Our plans were made, a movie camera was on hand, and the announcements were printed. I was diligently preparing a sermon for Sunday on the subject of "Adoption into God's Family."

Then the news came: Sara Elizabeth could not come to her new home this week. A small legal error was made in court, which prevented it. I hung up the phone and left my office to go home and share the disappointing news with Margaret. It was such a difficult day.

Each such experience is hard to take, but it's not the end of the world—not even the end of the road! Here are some observations I use that lift me when I'm disappointed:

1. Disappointments are only *delays.*

Who says that every setback must be final? What cannot be enjoyed today will possibly be yours tomorrow. Reshuffle your plans. Anticipation is as much fun as arrival. With the delay you have more time to plan and become excited.

2. Disappointments are *instructional.*

Many times a person can learn from a setback. Valuable lessons freely flow our way when our plans are denied or postponed.

3. Disappointments are just *stop signs.*

There are times when evaluation is necessary in each of our lives. Perhaps the promotion that was expected but did not materialize will encourage you to consider another avenue toward the top. Remember—the road to success is uphill *all* the way.

4. Disappointments are times of *adjustment.*

Too many times life becomes routine and boring. Schedules can become too rigid and unexciting. Some of your greatest moments can be times when you're forced out of that rut because of a turn of events. When you're forced to adjust your plans, begin to look for a fresh idea, a new friend, and a better day.

Some of your greatest moments can be times when you're forced out of that rut because of a turn of events.

5. Disappointments are *preventives.*

When a setback occurs, it's good to take a brief moment to analyze the reason for it. Often ineffective communication, insufficient resources, and a lack of planning cause an individual to fall short of the goals desired. Thorough preparation will eliminate many disappointments.

6. Disappointments are *pacesetters.*

Athletes are discouraged when an injury does not heal as quickly as desired. That type of a setback is for the good of the ball player. The pain of the injury is setting the pace for his or her body to heal properly. You may need some type of a roadblock to be placed in front of your progress so that your physical, emotional, or spiritual well-being can become properly balanced for the road you're to travel.

7. Disappointments are merely *obstacles.*

Ever since Adam and Eve disobeyed God, humanity has not had an easy life. Thorns grow beside the rose. Weeds spring up in the garden. Clouds hide the sunshine, and disappointments cloud our days. But remember—this is the way life is. Capitalize on these experiences.

8. Disappointments are *indicators.*

Disappointments sometimes indicate that problems loom ahead. Disappointments may indicate that adjustments of our priorities need to be made. Most important of all, how you react toward disappointments that cross your way will indicate what kind of a person you are and will become. How you act toward life shows what type of a person you want to be. How you react toward life shows what type of person you are right now.

9. Disappointments are *necessary*.

For total development, different kinds of experiences must come your way. There's no possible way that the fruit of maturity can be in evidence in your life without your experiencing disappointments. Some of life's greatest virtues—such as faith, patience, perseverance, and hope—come by way of disappointments. Only then will you realize that every problem in life has a solution. Only then will you have the important ingredients within your character to seek that solution instead of being perplexed by the problem.

Some of life's greatest virtues—such as faith, patience, perseverance, and hope—come by way of disappointments.

10. Disappointments are *tests*.

The greatest test for your character is what it takes to stop you. Successful people realize that the door to the room of success swings on the hinges of setbacks and opposition. The most noticeable difference between those who achieve and those who fail is seen in the area of perseverance. *Every-*

one has disappointments. *Every person* faces roadblocks. The one who succeeds is the one who will not quit.

11. Disappointments are *motivators.*

There are times in our lives when we become apathetic and listless. There is seemingly no motivation. Sometimes disappointments stun us and shake our lives until there is aroused in us an eager desire to spring out of our apathy into action. My motivation to become a soul winner began when a friend whom I had failed to share my faith with died. Suddenly, through that disappointment, I was motivated to change my entire ministry and place at the top of my priority list the winning of others to Christ.

12. Disappointments are *eliminators.*

Sometimes we have our hearts set on the wrong things, and what we regard as misfortunes may be the very means of making possible that which could otherwise not be achieved. Just as it's important for a successful mountain climber to eliminate all dead weight, it's needful for us to have many unnecessary priorities eliminated from our lives in order that we might climb to the top.

> *Sometimes we have our hearts set on the wrong things, and what we regard as misfortunes may be the very means of making possible that which could otherwise not be achieved.*

Disappointments many times consume these unimportant weights that would hold us back.

13. Disappointments are *normal.*

Disappointments alone don't have a positive or negative impact of themselves. By our reaction toward disappointments, we make them either positive or negative. Two people can have the same disappointment with a totally different outcome. It's how we handle the setbacks in our lives that will determine our success.

14. Disappointments are one of life's *trials.*

Hebrews 12:11 says, "No discipline seems pleasant at the time, but painful. Later on, however, it produces a harvest of righteousness and peace for those who have been trained by it." In other words, how happy are tried Christians afterward! Victory banquets are for soldiers home from war. After killing the lion, we eat the honey. If we can sing in the dungeon, how much more beautifully will we sing in heaven!

15. Disappointments are *stepping-stones.*

The king of the mountain stands upon stones of difficulty and opposition. Victorious is that person who knows how to make stepping-stones out of stumbling stones. As each stone is placed on our pathway to the top, it either becomes a help or a hindrance, depending upon how we handle each situation. Climb on top of each stone and go higher toward victory.

23

OPPORTUNITY OFTEN KNOCKS TWICE

In the days before modern harbors, a ship would sometimes have to wait until flood tide before it could make it into port. The term for this in Latin was *ob porter,* which signifies a ship standing over against a port waiting for the moment when it can ride the turn of the tide into the harbor.

The English word "opportunity" is derived from this original meaning. The captain and the crew were ready and waiting for that one moment, for they knew that if they missed it, they would have to wait for another tide to come in.

Shakespeare turned the background of the exact meaning of the word "opportunity" into one of his most famous passages:

> *There is a tide in the affairs of men,*
> *Which, taken at the flood, leads on to fortune;*
> *Omitted, all the voyage of their life*
> *Is bound in shallows and in miseries.*
> *On such a full sea are we now afloat;*
> *And we must take the current when it serves,*
> *Or lose our ventures.*

Without question, we must move quickly when the tide is high to sweep us into the harbor. Delay will keep us from our objective. Yet I am not totally convinced that all is lost if we allow an opportunity to pass us by without seizing it. Opportunities, like tides, will often come again to give us a second chance to achieve our goal. Opportunity can be ours the second time.

1. *Opportunity comes more than once if we're patient.*

Just as the tide comes and goes, so do opportunities. Often after missing an opportunity, I have tried the principle of patience. Try to create the same atmosphere that was present when opportunity first knocked. Become mentally prepared during this time of waiting so that opportunity will not pass you by again.

2. *Opportunities come more than once if we look for them.*

I'm convinced that opportunities are always surrounding people. It's not lack of opportunities that's the problem, but the inability to see these precious opportunities and thus miss them. Opportunities for success in this world are as great as we have the imagination to dream them, but we can't see them when we're down on ourselves and the world.

Opportunities for success in this world are as great as we have the imagination to dream them, but we can't see them when we're down on ourselves and the world.

When I was a youngster, I enjoyed going to the city park before Easter to join the other kids in the town's annual Easter egg hunt. The first year I went I learned a valuable lesson. Before the hunt began, I spotted an egg under a bush. I set my sights on that egg and quickly ran toward it when the race began. Another boy saw it also—and beat me to it. I stood there disappointed, thinking I had blown my chance.

While I was standing looking at the ground, other kids were scurrying around finding other eggs. I had allowed that one missed opportunity to keep me from looking for other eggs. Instead of a basketful of eggs, I went home empty-handed. Why? I failed to realize that there were a lot more eggs in the park just waiting to be picked up by those who saw them.

Inventors fail many times yet realize that the longer they work, the more they study, and the closer they look, the greater their chances for success.

What are inventors? People who see opportunity in things where others see nothing—people whose senses are alive to creative possibilities. Inventors fail many times yet realize that the longer they work, the more they study, and the closer they look, the greater their chances for success.

3. *Opportunity comes more than once if we constantly knock on its door.*

Opportunity is not mere chance or a freak happening. You must often make your own opportunities. A study was made of 400 eminent men and women of this century. The researchers concluded that three-fourths of these celebrated people had been handicapped in their youth by tragedies, disabilities, or great frustrations and had overcome those problems to achieve their positions of renown and make their contributions to others. Don't feel sorry for yourself if you're limited in your abilities and talents. The world is full of opportunities behind closed doors, so start knocking.

4. *Opportunities come more than once if we're willing to try other avenues to reach our goal.*

Perhaps you missed the first tide; is there another? Maybe you should try a different harbor altogether. Is there not more than one way to climb the mountain to success? Don't be discouraged or feel your chances for happiness are gone forever. Sit down, analyze, plan, and then move toward your goal by traveling another road.

Basketball was very important to me when I was growing up. During the summer, the players went to a camp for a couple of weeks to learn and to develop their skills. I was unable to go to camp because of other commitments. I felt certain that the missed opportunity would hurt my chances for making the starting lineup. Instead of crying over a missed opportunity, I developed another plan. I worked out twice a day all summer to make up for my absence at camp. My strategy worked!

What's your strategy when opportunity escapes you? Remember—there will be another chance if you're patient, looking, knocking, and willing to travel another path to reach the same goal.

24

PERSISTENCE PAYS

As stated in the previous chapter, in my younger days basketball was my first love. Many of my favorite memories are connected with the sound of a basketball bouncing upon our cement driveway at home. The older I became, the more my love for the game increased. When I was old enough to enter competitive sports and try out for the team at school, I made the team! Much to my surprise, the first three weeks of ball practice were spent doing strenuous exercises. Running sprints, jumping, and more running took up all our practice time. Each day there were fewer kids coming to practice. The coach would continually say, "Men, I not only want to see you physically in shape—I also want to measure your heart." Today I understand what he meant. Victory does not usually go to the most skilled. Victory is usually won by those who are the most persistent.

Regardless of the goal, a persistent effort is one of the most important ingredients for personal success. Napoleon Hill, author of *Think and Grow Rich,* studied the lives of more than 500 successful people in America and knew many of them personally. He discovered that the one indispensable ingredient common to all of them was *persistence.* These individuals kept trying even after repeated failures. It almost seems that great success is won only by people who overcome incredible obstacles and great discouragement.

If persistence is so rewarding, why are there so many people who become discouraged and give up?

Out of Hill's study comes this important truth: Success is achieved and maintained by those who keep trying. In other words, *persistence pays!*

If persistence is so rewarding, why are there so many people who become discouraged and give up? Although there are many reasons, let's examine just five of them:

1. **Many people do not persist because *they're uncertain what it is they really desire.***

Perhaps you decide to learn a foreign language, study music, begin a new career, or train yourself physically. Will your venture be a success or a failure? It depends upon how much pluck and perseverance that word "decide" contains. Having the confidence that nothing can overcome us and having a grip that nothing can detach *will* bring success. James says, "A double minded man is unstable in all his ways" (James 1:8, KJV). If you don't greatly desire what you decide upon, the wave of opposition will quickly come and wash you away from your halfhearted purpose.

2. **People sometimes quit because *they don't "feel gratified."***

One of the most common mistakes and the most costly is for a person to think that success is due to some genius, some magic formula that a few people have discovered and applied. Success is generally the result of holding on, and failure results in letting go. Ability is 90 percent "*stick*ability"!

3. **Often persistence wanes *when there seemingly is no hope.***

When clouds of discouragement begin to obscure the dreams of victory, the situation becomes crucial. The test of persistence does not occur when an individual already senses victory and hears the crowd cheer. That's the *result* of persistence. The true test of persistence comes when the

The line between failure and success is so fine that we scarcely know when we pass it.

night is the darkest. Only when the answers fade away, leaving only problems, and when the moral support of others disappears and loneliness becomes our partner can the strength of our persistence be determined.

The line between failure and success is so fine that we scarcely know when we pass it. There may often be times when we're on the line and don't know it. Many an individual has thrown up his or her hands at a time when a little more effort, a little more patience would have brought success. As the tide goes all the way out, so, too, does it come all the way in. Sometimes, prospects may seem dimmest just when they're on the turn. A little more persistence, a little more effort, and what seemed a hopeless failure may turn into a glorious success.

4. Many fail because *they're unwilling to pay the price for victory.*

A distance runner learns to depend upon his or her "second wind." There comes a time while running that the runner feels that he or she can run no farther. Instead of giving in to this feeling, the runner continues to run. Soon the bad feelings subside, and the runner gets his or her "second wind." This truth can be applied to any person's life. Until an individual tries hard enough and long enough, he or she never knows how much can be accomplished.

5. People sometimes lose determination because *they have not tasted many victories.*

Nothing develops persistence like a few victories. Losers often lose simply because they're unaware of the joy of winning. They've quit so many times that they've become accustomed to failure. This truth is illustrated in a poem titled "Perseverance."

> *Two frogs fell into a can of cream,*
>   *Or so I've heard it told.*
> *The sides of the can were shiny and steep;*
>   *The cream was deep and cold.*
>
> *"Oh, what's the use?" said No. 1,*
>   *"'Tis fate—no help's around.*
> *Good-bye, my friend! Good-bye, sad world!"*
>   *And, weeping still, he drowned.*
>
> *But No. 2, of sterner stuff,*
>   *Dog-paddled in surprise,*
> *The while he wiped his creamy face*
>   *And dried his creamy eyes.*

"I'll swim awhile, at least," he said—
Or so I've heard it said—
"It wouldn't really help the world,
If one more frog was dead."

An hour or two he kicked and swam.
Not once he stopped to mutter,
But kicked and swam, and swam and kicked,
Then hopped out via butter!
—T. C. Hamlett

25

SUCCESSFUL FAILURE

In our lifetime most of us have had a variety of experiences that would be classified as failures. The frustration, hurt, or disappointment that we sense when our goals are not met is a feeling common to all of us. Perhaps it's the feelings about failure that cause many to begin to fear failure. Maybe our dread of failure stems from the misconception that failure is final. There are times when apparent failure is not failure at all if we remember the principles that turn failure into success.

1. *An experience is not a failure if it prods us to keep on trying.*

The line between failure and success is so fine that we scarcely know when we pass it. In fact, we're often on that line and don't realize it. Many a person has thrown up his or her hands at a time when, with a little more effort and patience, he or she would have achieved success. As the tide goes clear out—so it comes clear in. There is no failure except in no longer trying. There is no failure except from within. There is no insurmountable barrier until we give up on our purpose.

Booker T. Washington said, "Success is to be measured not so much by the position that one has reached in life as by the obstacles which he has overcome while trying to succeed." Each person in life lives in one of two worlds. There is the crowded world of the defeated, who quit—and the roomy world of the succeeders, who persist.

One of the basic principles of the Christian faith is that God doesn't get discouraged, and therefore neither should we.

One of the basic principles of the Christian faith is that God doesn't get discouraged, and therefore neither should we. Many of the setbacks originally designed to finish us off can, if properly used, be the very things that bring us out on top.

I love the story of the mule who fell into an old dry well many feet deep. All efforts to rescue him were fruitless. Finally, the owner of the mule, supposing that the poor creature was severely injured by the fall, decided it would be more merciful to kill him than allow him to starve to death. Unable to think of a better way of dispatching him, he had a truckload of dirt thrown in onto him. Instead of allowing himself to be buried alive, the mule quickly shook off the dirt and pressed it down with his feet, thus raising himself a few inches above his original position. Another load was thrown into the well with the same result.

Slowly but surely, inch by inch, the mule ascended until the well was filled within a few feet of the top. Then, as complacently as if nothing strange had happened to him, the mule stepped out on firm, safe ground. It may offend a few people to look at a mule for a lesson in living. But some people have never learned what that mule already knew—that the very setback originally designed to finish a person off, when properly used, can become the thing that brings him or her out on top.

2. *An experience is not a failure if through it we discover how we failed and we put that knowledge to good use.*

D. H. Lawrence said, "If only we could have two lives—the first in which we make mistakes, and the second to profit by them." A discouraged young writer once heard these words: "Every one of your rejected manuscripts was rejected for a reason. Have you checked each failure and found why? You must put your failure to work for you."

The greatest mistake we ever make is not learning from and correcting the first one.

The greatest mistake we ever make is not learning from and correcting the first one.

3. *An experience is not a failure if through it we discover our own true selves.*

In the biographies of great men and women, it is evident that many successful people started out in life as failures, and because they failed they found themselves and their life's work.

When Nathaniel Hawthorne lost his position in the Custom House at Salem, Massachusetts, he came home utterly defeated and told his wife that he was a complete failure. To his amazement, she greeted his dismissal news with delight, saying, "Now you can write a book." So he sat down and wrote *The Scarlet Letter,* which is still considered by many critics as the greatest novel ever written in our country. James Whistler failed at West Point. After he was dropped from the list of students there, he halfheartedly tried engineering. Finally he tried painting, with the success that is well known. A great many people in every generation are unhappy failures for no other reason than that they've not found themselves or their proper vocation. And if because of failure a person finally discovers where and how his or her talents can best be used for God, the failure must surely be regarded a success.

4. *An experience is not a failure if through it we become better-disciplined individuals.*

The New Testament has much to say about disciplined living. In 2 Corinthians the apostle Paul compares life to a footrace between two disciplined, well-trained athletes. Great men have had failure, struggle, and discipline woven into their lives. If our experiences in life, however bitter or unfortunate, mellow our hearts, humble our spirits, purify our motives, cleanse our souls, and make us more sensitive to proper values and more sympathetic toward the unfortunate, then we will have succeeded.

In summary, if we use our so-called failures as instruments to discipline our inner spirits, they are not really failures, but successes!

Part IV
LOOK OUT FOR YOUR OUTLOOK

26

HAS YOUR EXPECTER EXPIRED?

My friend Joe Sawyer tells a cute story about a boy who was fishing one day. An elderly man who was fishing nearby noticed that the young lad was having considerable success in his endeavor. What was more unusual than the amount of fish he would catch was what he would do with the fish once they were successfully landed on the bank. The boy would hold each fish up to his hand and measure it. If the fish was larger than his hand, he would throw it back into the water. He kept only the small ones.

Finally curiosity motivated the old man to slip over to the young boy and ask, "Son, why do you keep the small fish and throw the large ones back into the water?"

The young boy replied, "I can't keep the big ones—I only have a 10-inch frying pan!"

I'm afraid there are a lot of people shortchanging themselves because they're limited to a 10-inch frying pan. They think no bigger, see no bigger, act no bigger, and expect no bigger! Instead of expanding their horizons by enlarging their expectations, they reduce their potential by shrinking their hopes. Too many people fail to realize that their expectation measures the height of their future possibilities. It's impossible to achieve success without expecting it.

Many people are not receiving miracles in their lives because their "expecter" has expired. Once they had dreams; now they have doubts. The future looked bright; now it looks bleak. Better days ahead have been clouded by bitter days behind. They're in trouble. If this has happened to you, revitalize your expecter by adopting the following principles:

1. *Your life must be influenced by your expectations, not your experience.*

People's lives are often guided by some dramatic experience of the past. Tragically, they never gain any new ground because they're prisoners to past problems. They frequently comment, "I tried that once, and it failed" or "You can't teach an old dog new tricks" or "It's always been done this way." These individuals have made the terrible mistake of believing that things never change and that experience is the best teacher—it gives the test first and the lesson afterward.

To limit our lives to our past experiences is to cheat ourselves from developing our potential and increasing our possibilities for success. Mark Twain said, "If a cat sits on a hot stove, it will never sit on a hot stove again. Of course, it will never sit on a cold one either." Forget your past failures and begin to enlarge your expectations for tomorrow.

To limit our lives to our past experiences is to cheat ourselves from developing our potential and increasing our possibilities for success.

2. *Your life must be influenced by your expectations, not by others' examples.*

We all have someone we admire. At times it's tempting to try to imitate them. That's why I feel it's important for our country to produce heroes who live by Christian principles. Have you asked yourself lately, "Where have all the good heroes gone?" The danger in patterning our lives after others is that too often we forget that they're human. Their feet are made of clay, and they're susceptible to failures just like we are. Their valleys possibly could become yours.

Their stumblings might limit your ascent to the top of the mountain.

3. *Your life must be influenced by your expectations, not by your exhilaration.*

Moods of people vary to a great degree. At times during a mood of joy and happiness, decisions are made that are not in a person's best interest. Decisions should be made based on evidence and sound reasoning, not made during moments of emotional high tide. Your emotions are created by too many unstable factors in life. The world is run by people who don't "feel like it." No other area in your life will reveal your discipline more than your ability to conquer your moodiness and to rely heavily upon your expectations.

Take a moment to inspect your expecter. Your expectations must not be based on what you are today, but on what you hope to become someday. Your expecter must be energized, because it's the key that unlocks the door to many miracles. We're taught in the Word that "you do not have because you do not ask" (James 4:2, NKJV). Most of the time you ask not because you expect not. Your asking will increase with boldness to the degree that your expectations increase. In other words, energize your expecter, and expect to win.

27

WHICH TENT DO YOU LIVE IN?

All persons live in one of two tents—content or discontent. In which do *you* live?

The contented person looks beyond circumstances and sees a better day; the discontented person looks at circumstances and sees no other way.

The contented person understands the purpose for which he or she was born; the discontented person looks at others' success with a face filled with scorn.

The contented person has surrendered to a purpose that demands his or her best; the discontented person has selfishly hoarded much and, grasping for more, will not rest.

The contented person has placed his or her values on things that will forever last; the discontented person has placed his or her values on things that will soon be past.

The contented person is anchored to clear goals and is hardly ever swayed; the discontented person has no goals that anchor him or her and is many times dismayed.

The contented person counts his or her blessings and names them one by one; the discontented person counts others' blessings and thinks he or she has no fun.

All persons live in one of two tents—content or discontent. In which tent do you live?

28

T.G.I.M.!
(THANK GOODNESS,
IT'S MONDAY!)

I was talking with an employee of a motel where I was staying for a few days. After a brief conversation, she exclaimed, "Thank goodness, it's Friday! You won't see me again until Monday!" She went down the hallway counting the hours until her work would be finished and the weekend would begin.

I suppose a lot of people are happy when the week rolls around to Friday. It's great to leave problems and demands behind, knowing that the next couple of days are yours. Yet I often ask myself, "Why should Monday be so blue?" When I go into my staff meeting next Monday morning, I'm going to stand up, throw back my head, and say, "Thank goodness, it's Monday!"

There are several reasons why I say, "T.G.I.M.!" First, I've discovered that the journey is as much fun as arriving at my destination. Anticipation is as exciting as realization—planning as delightful as producing. Christmas is fun long before December 25. Vacations are fun before I pack the car and say "good-bye" to the neighbors. Likewise, Monday is the beginning of a new venture—it's the start of another journey.

Monday morning is the only time I can stand up and say, "So far this week I haven't made a mistake."

Second, I say, "T.G.I.M.!" because I have the opportunity for a fresh, new start. Last week's mistakes can be corrected this week. Last week's sorrow can become this week's joy. I have another chance to do right. Monday morning is the only time I can stand up and say, "So far this week I haven't made a mistake." It's the day I can write on a clean sheet of paper all the things I want to accomplish for the entire week. Mondays remind me of the day Christ forgave all the sins I had committed. Oh, the joy of having all my sins washed away, forgiven and forgotten—my slate completely wiped clean through the precious blood of Jesus! Forgiveness and Mondays give me a brand-new start.

Third, Monday gives me an opportunity to dream new dreams and set new goals. Many goals are not reached in a day. If I start running on Monday morning, perhaps I'll arrive at my designated destination by the end of the week—or month.

And, fourth, Monday is the day I enter into the arena of action. It's time to see if my game plan will really work. I played competitive basketball when I was in school and can still remember the thrill of beginning a new game. As I stood around the center circle waiting for the opening tip-off, a certain excitement would jump up and down my spine that was not the same at any other time. All the wind sprints, strategy sessions, endless drills, scrimmages, and pep rallies were for *this* moment. This was the time for action. Would all the sweat, plans, discipline, and coaching be sufficient for this moment? Now was the moment of truth! Monday is like the opening tip-off of a basketball game. It's the day to experience the thrill of new action.

Last, I say, "T.G.I.M.!" also because I'm reminded that life is really giving and loving. On the weekend I have lived for myself. I have indulged in doing "my thing" and have almost forgotten my responsibilities. Monday morning I'm awakened to the fact that no individual is an island. The greatest joys in life come to us when we serve others.

Monday helps me keep my priorities straight. It's the day I can begin to help others. I can begin to anticipate the opportunities I'll be given to reach out a helping hand and give hope to someone in need. It's the beginning of a week that will allow me the opportunity to encourage, strengthen, counsel, and lift someone else. Monday is the day I have the chance to practice the teachings of Christ and experience the joy of serving others.

29

WHAT IS A PROBLEM?

Every year I spend hundreds of hours counseling many different people. They come from all types of environments. Their ages and intellects are different. They don't look alike, and certainly their personalities are not of the same mold. Yet there's something they all possess. Each person is driven to my office by a force called a "problem." Sometimes I recognize the problem before it becomes crucial. At other times, I'm the last resort. When all else has failed, it's time to talk to the pastor. Often they come into the office knowing the answer and just needing assurance and security. Occasionally they aren't even sure what the problem is.

While praying one day for a number of people with various difficulties, I found myself asking, "What are problems, and what can we do about them?" Can we solve them, or just relieve them, climb over them, eradicate them, or even ignore them? Problems keep popping up. I notice that when they arise, some people rise higher and become greater, while others fall deeper into the depths of discouragement. Problems are many things to many people, but I decided to look at them through the eyes of those who come out on top.

Remember—the circumstances in which we find ourselves today are a direct reflection of the decisions we made yesterday.

Problems are *predictors*. They forecast the future by exposing the trends of today. How you react to difficulty when it begins to surface will determine where you and that problem will be tomorrow. No trial will leave you tomorrow where you are today. The decisions we make today concerning problems we have will shape our future. Remember—the circumstances in which we find ourselves today are a direct reflection of the decisions we made yesterday.

Problems are *reminders*. They remind us that we need God's help to handle the upheavals of life. If instead of his confident statement "I can do everything through him who gives me strength" (Phil. 4:13), the apostle Paul had said, "I can do all things," his words would have sounded arrogant and his life would have been disappointing. Paul knew the secret of success was not self-confidence but *Christ*-confidence. His achievements could only come through Christ, and he succeeded because in every problem he remembered this truth.

Problems are *obstacles*. They frustrate us while we attempt to reach specific goals. A toddler handles most obstacles by crying. I know older people who pout, quit, blame somebody, or just try to ignore the whole situation. Regardless of our reaction to a problem, for a time it's an obstacle in our path.

Problems are *blessings*. They try us until we become stronger in our voyage through life. A smooth sea never made a skillful mariner. Fletcher Spruce wrote an article titled "Every Dog Needs a Few Fleas." As a child, he noticed the different temperaments of dogs. He observed that the active dogs had fleas and were always busy scratching. The lazy dogs had no fleas and therefore became very indolent. Obviously his conclusion was that every dog needed a few fleas to keep it alert, awake, and useful.

Problems are lessons. They teach us to be flexible yet determined.

Just as a few fleas are good for dogs, a few problems and tensions are good for us. The psalmist wrote, "It was good for me to be afflicted" (Ps. 119:71).

Problems are *lessons*. They teach us to be flexible yet determined. Many of these lessons can be taught only through trial and error. This course of study is labeled "experience." Experience is a hard teacher, who gives the test first and the lesson afterward. Experience is yesterday's answer to today's problems.

This course of study is labeled "experience."

Problems are *everywhere*. They are no respecter of persons, places, or time. Sooner or later a person, if he or she is wise, discovers that life is a mixture of good and bad days, victory and defeat, give and take. He or she learns that it doesn't pay to be too sensitive a soul, that it's best to let some things go over one's head like water off a duck's back. He or she learns that the person who loses his or her temper usually loses out, that all people have burned toast for breakfast now and then, and that it's best not to take our problems too seriously.

Problems are *messages*. They forecast what may possibly become a reality farther down the road. They are indicators measuring progress and development. They are communicators letting us know vital information. Sometimes they yell for attention. Sometimes they point for redirection. They can never be ignored. Sit back and analyze every problem and read the message it's sending. Then respond appropriately.

Problems are *solvable*. They always have an answer. Perhaps the answer is hidden, but *there is an answer.* The difficulty lies not so much in not finding the answer but in being unwilling to pay the price for solving it. I recently came across the following terse verse:

> *From the day of your birth*
> *'Til you ride in your hearse,*
> *Things are never so bad*
> *That they couldn't be worse!*

30

SING IN THE
SHOWER ANYWAY

Do you ever sing in the shower? If you're like me, you usually sing just a few measures and then stop. Why? It seems a little ridiculous to sing in the shower. What if someone heard you? If you shower in the morning, isn't it too early to be happy? Besides, you really can't carry a decent tune. You don't know all the words. You might wake someone up. All of a sudden, that inward impulse that prompted you to begin the day singing is crushed. Already you've allowed yourself to be shortchanged.

Too many times we allow outward circumstances and influences to control our actions and mold our thinking. Too often we limit our happiness by submitting to the constant pressures all around us. It's vitally important to realize that either the situations around us control our lives, or we control them. As someone said, "We don't sing because we're happy—we're happy because we sing." Indeed, we can create our own environment. We can make the bed in which we lie. We can "color our own world."

Have you ever known someone who could walk into a room full of people and in a few short moments completely change the atmosphere? How about that person who seemingly keeps his or her head above water while everyone else is drowning in confusion? Do you know people who, while others are bitter and critical, smile and spread love? What's their secret? They've learned to control their situation. They've realized that the outlook on their world depends upon doing what's right, not what's easy. They've learned that while conditions are not always favorable, they must "sing in the shower" anyway. The following characteristics are evident in such people:

1. They face each day with joy and optimism.

2. Their radiant lives draw others around them like a magnet.

3. They're always doing while most are doubting.

4. They never wait for favorable conditions to accomplish something worthwhile.

5. They always lift the spirits of those around them.

6. They work while others worry.

7. They're always discovering more potential within their own lives.

8. They make things happen while others wait for things to happen.

9. They initiate good thinking and positive action in an atmosphere of doubt and discouragement.

10. They're "lucky" because they're always coming out on top.

Stop for a moment! Where are you right now? Are you sitting on a heap of ashes feeling sorry for yourself? Are you drowning in a pool of problems? Are you slowly being buried by the pressures of life? If so, it's time to pick yourself up, walk toward the shower—and start singing!

31

GIVE TILL IT FEELS GOOD

There are two types of people when it comes to the matter of giving: Some give to live, while others live to give. These two types of individuals not only have very different giving habits but also have different philosophies.

For example, the person who gives to live will never do something for anyone without expecting a reward. This type of person always keeps a record of what he or she gives and receives. This type of person's only reward comes when he or she receives more than what was given.

Contrast that attitude with the individual who lives to give. This person expects neither reward nor payment and many times is offended if offered compensation. Such an individual does not judge a giving situation by what he or she will receive in return. His or her judgment is based on the question "Has this helped the person or cause in need?"

The person who gives to live will always be asking, "How much do I have to give?"

The person who gives to live will always be asking, "How much do I have to give?" His or her goal is to give "just enough." This type of person majors on the minimum.

The person who lives to give will always be asking, "How much more is needed to meet the need?" Often he or she will respond again and again to the same need until it is fully met. His or her interest is in solving the problem and filling the need. This type of person majors on the *maximum.*

Usually the person who gives to live strongly desires recognition. Often this person's giving will be determined by how much recognition he or she receives. This kind of individual very seldom works alone. He or she finds it hard to do a kind deed when the crowd is gone. In the parable of the Good Samaritan, I have no doubt that the priest and the Levite who passed the man in distress many times helped other people. Surely they had many times performed good deeds. Why did they not stop to help this man? Because this was a lonely road and no one would see them. The audience was absent.

And if assistance were given, there would be little chance of reward.

Recognition is not the motivation for giving when you live to give. At times, recognition will come to anyone who gives, yet this is not the primary factor in giving. Some never turn their heads to see who is looking and never wait to find out what the reward will be. This type of a person does much of his or her sharing in a quiet, private way.

At times, recognition will come to anyone who gives, yet this is not the primary factor in giving.

I know a wonderful man and his wife who do many nice things for people. There are times when they ask me to tell the person in need that his or her problem has been solved. But they also request that I not tell the needy individual that he or she is responsible for the gift. Why? Because the reward is in meeting other people's problems and not in receiving recognition.

The philosophy of "I give to live" is basically selfish. People who live by this philosophy are saying, "I wish it were possible to live and not give." If it were possible, they would never give. No matter how much they possess, it's never enough. One of their great concerns is "How much do I have left?" They're always afraid that their giving will bankrupt them either physically or financially. They have not yet come to the realization that this is an impossibility. They measure their success by the possessions that are theirs.

The philosophy of "I live to give" is a Christian philosophy. God was the perfect Example of this philosophy when He gave the world His only Son. Jesus emphasized this type of thinking when He said, "Love

The Christian life is saturated by giving.

your enemies, bless those who curse you, do good to those who hate you, and pray for those who spitefully use you and persecute you" (Matt. 5:44, NKJV). The Christian life is saturated by giving.

The person who "gives to live" is very seldom happy. The reasons are obvious. His or her motives are wrong; therefore, his or her reward is not enough. Such a person is selfish and is always afraid of receiving the "short end of the stick."

Now look at the person who lives to give. His or her only dissatisfaction comes when there seems to be no need to meet. This person is truly happiest when giving! Why? Because the giving is done with the right motive. The delight is in helping others. A smile of appreciation, an expression of hope, or a sigh of relief is reward enough. God's Word describes this type of individual as a "cheerful giver" (2 Cor. 9:7). If his or her giving has not caused some sacrifice, then he or she has not given enough. This type of person realizes that there's a point that must be passed before giving becomes a joy. We must pass the point of selfishness, greed, and personal desire. When we pass that important barrier, we begin to live for others and not for ourselves. Only then are we flooded with indescribable joy and happiness. Why? Because we've given till it feels good!

32

I WANT A "HOME ON THE RANGE"

One day my second grade teacher taught a song to my class, which I immediately enjoyed. It was titled "Home on the Range." The words are familiar:

> *Oh, give me a home where the buffalo roam,*
> *Where the deer and the antelope play,*
> *Where seldom is heard a discouraging word,*
> *And the skies are not cloudy all day.*
> —Brewster Higley

I've decided that's where I want to live. As soon as I can find that place, I'm going to move to my own "home on the range," where there seldom is heard a discouraging word. You can have the buffalo, deer, and antelope. I just want to live in an atmosphere that has eliminated discouraging words!

I've traveled and lived in the North American West, but I'm sure that's not the place. Out there on that range I've heard plenty of discouraging words. Can you help me? Do you know the place the song was written about? Allow me to share with you what discouragement by word, attitude, or action does to people.

Discouragement . . .

> keeps us from becoming what God intends for us
>
> hides the beauties of life from our lives
>
> smothers our ambitions
>
> shoves us into the crowds of losers
>
> flickers our light, which should shine brightly for Jesus
>
> identifies us with failure
>
> causes doubts to control our actions
>
> freezes our creative minds
>
> paralyzes our faith
>
> magnifies our problems
>
> clogs our positive influence on others

forces us to become introvertive

clouds our vision

dashes our dreams

Discouragement is a terrible hindrance to effective living. It's Satan's most effective tool, for it causes people to throw up their hands and quit. Although it's impossible to live in an atmosphere totally divorced from discouragement, there are a few positive steps that can be taken to help us be victorious while discouragement surrounds us. Here's a formula for conquering discouragement:

Add up all the successes of the past. Too many times when we're discouraged, we forget the past victories. Discouragement has a tendency to make us wallow in the muck of negative thinking until we think only of failure. We say to ourselves, "I'm no good" or "I'm always making mistakes" or

If your friends are tearing you down, it's better to find new ones or walk alone with God.

"Why can't I ever do anything right?" and so on. Stop dwelling in the night of negativism. Allow the light of victory to shine into your dungeon of discouragement.

Subtract all of your discouraging influences. Perhaps you have friends like Job's friends. Maybe they hinder you instead of help you. Take a piece of paper and make a list of your friends. Now write down their characteristics. Are your friends negative or positive? Do they lift you up or let you down? Do they possess such attitudes as envy, jealousy, anger, and bitterness? What do they like to talk about? If your friends are tearing you down, it's better to find new ones or walk alone with God. Begin reading good literature that will build your faith. Eliminate anything from your life that has a tendency to keep you discouraged.

Multiply all of God's promises to you. Allow me to share just one of God's many promises. Isaiah 43:1-3 reads, "But now, this is what the LORD says—he who created you, O Jacob, he who formed you, O Israel: 'Fear not, for I have redeemed you; I have summoned you by name; you are mine. When you pass through the waters, I will be with you; and when you pass through the rivers, they will not sweep over you. When you walk through the fire, you will not be burned; the flames will not set you ablaze. For I am the LORD, your God, the Holy One of Israel, your Savior.'"

Divide up all of God's blessings to you, and give them out to others. There is no more effective way of overcoming discouragement than by sharing something good with someone. One of the major causes of discouragement is self-pity. When we begin to forget ourselves by reaching out to others, a spirit of usefulness and encouragement invades our lives.

Let's not put our house up for sale and go looking for a "home on the range." The grass need not be greener on the other side. Right now, decide right where you live that you're going to be an encourager, an uplifter, and a helper. Soon people will be saying they want to live beside you and become acquainted with you and be your friend. Why? Because when they are around *you*, there "seldom is heard a discouraging word."

33

HOPE—HOLDING ON, PRAYING EXPECTANTLY

I listened patiently as he poured out his problems. His work was not going well. Some of his children were sowing their wild oats, and he was worried about them. The straw that finally broke his back was when his wife decided to leave him. There he sat, all slumped over in despair. It was the last sentence of his story that alarmed me. He said, "I have nothing to live for—I've lost all hope."

I began to share with him that hope was the one thing he could not afford to lose. He could lose his business, his money, and maybe even his family, and rebound on the court of life if he kept his hope alive.

If hope is so important, what is it? Tertullian said, "Hope is patience with the lamp lit." Hope is holding on when things around you begin to slip away. Hope is praying expectantly when there seemingly are no answers. G. Campbell Morgan tells of a man whose shop burned during the disastrous Chicago fire. He arrived at the ruins the next morning carrying a table. He set the table amid the charred debris and above it placed this optimistic sign: "Everything lost except wife, children, and hope. Business will be resumed as usual tomorrow morning."

The only difference between those who threw in the towel and quit and those who used their energy to rebuild and kept going is found in the word "hope."

Many men and women become bitter toward life because of the unfortunate circumstances in which they find themselves. Many quit. Others have taken their own lives. What makes the difference in the outcome? Talent? No! The only difference between those who threw in the towel and quit and those who used their energy to rebuild and kept going is found in the word "hope."

What does hope do for humanity?

Hope shines brightest when the hour is darkest.

Hope motivates when discouragement comes.

Hope energizes when the body is tired.

Hope sweetens while the bitterness bites.

Hope sings when all melodies are gone.

Hope believes when the evidence is eliminated.

Hope listens for answers when no one is talking.

Hope climbs over obstacles when no one is helping.

Hope endures hardship when no one is caring.

Hope smiles confidently when no one is laughing.

Hope reaches for answers when no one is asking.

Hope presses toward victory when no one is encouraging.

Hope dares to give when no one is sharing.

Hope brings the victory when no one is winning.

There's nothing to do but bury a person when his or her hopes are gone. Losing hope usually precedes loss of life itself. You don't need a better environment—you just need more hope. It's the one thing in your life you can't do without!

Our Vision

To see effective Christian leaders fulfill the Great Commission in every nation.

Our Mission

To equip international Christian leaders to effectively serve the growing Body of Christ around the world.

Our Process

To provide strategic leadership training through conferences, resources, partnerships and technology.

Our Invitation

We invite you to invest your prayers, talents and financial resources with EQUIP to develop effective Christian leaders who will reach the nations for Christ.

Equipping Leaders To Reach Our World

PO Box 1808
Duluth, GA 30096
888.993.7847
www.iequip.org